Two War Years in Constantinople

Sketches of German and Young Turkish
Ethics and Politics (Including: The great
Armenian persecutions—The system of
Talaat and Enver)

Harry Stuermer

Two War Years in Constantinople: Sketches of German and Young Turkish Ethics and Politics (Including: The great Armenian persecutions—The system of Talaat and Enver)

Contact:
IndoEuropeanPublishing@gmail.com

The present edition is a reproduction of 1917 publication of this work, produced in the current edition with completely new, easy to read format by Indo-European Publishing.

For an authentic reading experience, the Spelling, punctuation, and capitalization have been retained from the original text.

Cover Design by Indo-European Design Team

ISBN: 978-1-60444-563-3

IndoEuropean
Publishing.com
Los Angeles, CA, USA

CONTENTS

At the outbreak of war in Germany—The German "world-politicians" (Weltpolitiker)—German and English mentality—The "place in the sun"—England's declaration of war—German methods in Belgium and Alsace-Lorraine — Prussian arrogance—Militaristic journalism

To Constantinople—Pro-Turkish considerations—The dilemma of a Gallipoli correspondent—Under German military control

The great Armenian persecutions—The system of Talaat and Enver—A denunciation of Germany as a cowardly and conscienceless accomplice

The tide of war—Enver's offensive for the "liberation of the Caucasus"—The Dardanelles Campaign; the fate of Constantinople twice hangs in the balance—Nervous tension in international Pera—Bulgaria's attitude—Turkish rancour against her former enemy—German illusions of a separate peace with Russia—King Ferdinand's time-serving—Lack of munitions in the Dardanelles—A mysterious death: a political murder?—The evacuation of Gallipoli—The Turkish version of victory—Constantinople unreleased—Kut-el-Amara—Propaganda foe the "Holy War"—A prisoner of repute—Loyalty of Anglo-Indian officers—Turkish communiques and their worth—The fall of Erzerum—Official lies—The treatment of prisoners— Political speculation with prisoners of war—Treatment of enemy subjects—Stagnation and lassitude in the summer of 1916—The Greeks in Turkey—Dread of Greek massacres—Rumania's entry—Terrible disappointment— The three phases of the war for Turkey

The economic situation—Exaggerated Entente hopes—Hunger and suffering among the civil population—The system of requisitioning and the semi-official monopolists—Profiteering on the part of the Government clique—Frivolity and cynicism—The "Djemiet"—The delegates of the German Zentrulinkaufagesellschaft (Central Purchases Commission)—A hard battle between German and Turkish intrigue—Reform of the coinage—Paper money and its depreciation—The hoarding of bullion—The Russian rouble the best investment

German propaganda and ethics—The unsuccessful "Holy War" and the German Government—"The Holy War" a crime against civilisation, a chimera, a farce—Underhand dealings—The German Embassy the dupe of adventurers—The morality of German Press representatives— A trusty servant of the German Embassy—Fine official distinctions of morality—The German conception of the rights of individuals

Anti-war and pro-Entente feelings among the Turks—
Turkish pessimism about the war—How would Abdul-
Hamid have acted?—A war of prevention against Russia—
Russia and a neutral Turkey—The agreement about the
Dardanelles —A peaceful solution scorned—Alleged
criminal intentions on the part of the Entente; the example of
Greece and Salonika—To be or not to be?—German
influence— Turkey stakes on the wrong card—The results

The outlook for the future—The consequences of trusting
Germany—The Entente's death sentence on Turkey— The
social necessity for this deliverance—Anatolia, the new
Turkey after the war; forecasts about the Turkish race—The
Turkish element in the lost territory—Russia and
Constantinople; international guarantees—Germany, at
peace, benefits too—Farewell to the German "World
Politicians"—German interests in a victorious and in a
defeated Turkey—The German-Turkish treaty—A paradise
on earth—The Russian commercial impulse—The new
Armenia Western Anatolia, the old Greek centre of
civilisation—Great Arabia and Syria—The reconciliation of
Germany

DECLARATION

The undersigned hereby declares on his sworn word of honour that in writing this volume he has been in no way inspired by outside influence, and that he has never had any dealings whatsoever, material or otherwise, either before or during the war, with any Government, organisation, propaganda, or personality hostile to Germany or Turkey or even of a neutral character. His conscience alone has urged him to write and publish his impressions, and he hopes that by so doing he may perform a service towards the cause of truth and civilisation.

Moreover, he can give formal assurance that he has expressly avoided making the acquaintance of any person resident in Switzerland until his manuscript should have been sent to press.

Furthermore, he has been actuated by no personal motives in thus giving public expression to his experiences and opinions, for he has no personal grievance, either material or moral, against any person whatsoever.

Geneva,
June 1917

PREFACE

While the author of this work was waiting on the frontier of Switzerland for final permission from the German authorities to enter that country, Germany committed her second great crime, her first having completely missed its mark. She had begun to realise that she was beaten in the great conflict which she had so wantonly provoked with that characteristic over confidence in the power of her own militarism and disdainful undervaluation of the morale and general capacities of her enemies. In final renunciation of any last remnants of humanity in her methods, she was now making a dying effort to help her already lost cause by a ruthless extension of her policy of piracy at sea and a gratification of all her brutal instincts in complete violation of the rights of neutral countries.

It is therefore with all the more inward conviction, with all the more urgent moral persuasion, that the author makes use of the rare opportunity offered him by residence in Switzerland to range himself boldly on the side of truth and show that there are still Germans who find it impossible to condone even tacitly the moral transgression and political stupidity of their own and an allied Government. That is the sole purpose of this publication.

Regardless of the consequences, he holds it to be his duty and his privilege, just because he is a German, to make a frank statement, from the point of view of human civilisation, of what have become his convictions from personal observations made in the course of six months of actual warfare and practically two years of subsequent journalistic activity. He spent the time from Spring 1915 to Christmas 1916 in Turkey, and will of course only deal with what he knows from personal observation. The following essays are of the nature merely of sketches and make no claim whatever to completeness.

With regard to purely German politics and ethics, therefore, the author will confine himself to a few indications and impressions of a personal kind, but he cannot forget the rôle Germany has played in Turkey as an ally of the present Young Turkish Government, nor can he ignore Germany's responsibility for the atrocities committed by them. The author publishes his impressions with a perfectly clear conscience, secure in the conviction that as the representative of a German paper he never once wrote a single word in favour of this criminal war, and that during his stay of more than twenty months in Turkey he never concealed his true opinions as soon as he had definitely made up his mind what these were.

On the contrary, he was rather dangerously candid and frank in speaking to anyone who wanted to listen to him—so much so, that it is almost a miracle that he ever reached a neutral country. After the war he will be in a position to appeal to the testimony of dozens of people of high standing in all walks of life that in both thought and action a deep cleft has always divided him from his colleagues, and that he has ever ardently longed for the moment when he might, freely and without fear of consequences, do his bit towards the enlightenment of the civilised world.

May these lines, written in all sincerity and hereby submitted to the tribunal of public opinion, free the author at last from the burden of silent reproach heaped on him by a mutilated, outraged, languishing humanity, of being a German among thousands of Germans who desired this war.

Several months have passed since the original text of the German and French editions of this little book was written. Baghdad was taken by British troops before the last chapter of the German manuscript had been completed, and since then military operations have been more and more in favour of the Entente. A number of important political events have occurred, such as the Russian Revolution and the entry of the United States of America into the war.

Further developments of Russian politics may yet have a direct effect on the final solution of the problems surrounding the defeated Ottoman Empire. But the author has preferred to maintain the original text of his book, written early in March this year, and to make no changes whatever in the conclusions he had then arrived at as a result of the fresh impressions he carried away from Turkey.

CHAPTER I

At the outbreak of war in Germany — The German "World-politicians" (Weltpolitiker) — German and English mentality — The "place in the sun" — England's declaration of war — German methods in Belgium and Alsace-Lorraine — Prussian arrogance — Militaristic journalism.

Anyone who, like myself, set foot on German soil for the first time after years of sojourn in foreign lands, and more particularly in the colonies, just at the moment that Germany was mobilising for the great European war, must surely have been filled, as I was, with a certain feeling of melancholy, a slight uneasiness with regard to the state of mind of his fellow-countrymen as it showed itself in these dramatic days of August in conversations in the street, in cafés and restaurants, and in the articles appearing in the Press. We Germans have never learnt to think soundly on political subjects. Bismarck's political heritage, although set forth in most popular form in his Thoughts and Recollections, a book that anyone opposing this war from the point of view rather of prudence than of ethics might utilise as an unending source of propaganda, has not descended to our rulers in any sort of living form. But an unbounded political naïveté, an incredible lack of judgment and of understanding of the point of view of other peoples, who have their raison d'être just as much as we have, their vital interests, their standpoint of honour — have not prevented us from trying to carry on a grand system of Weltpolitik (world politics). The average everyday German has never really understood the English — either before or during the war; in the latter's colonial policy, which, according to pan-German ideas, has no other aim than to snatch from us our "place in the sun"; in their conception of liberty and civilisation, which has entailed such mighty sacrifices for them on behalf of their Allies; when we trod Belgian neutrality underfoot and thought England would stand and look on; at the time of the debates about universal service, when practically every German, even in the highest

1

political circles, was ready to wager that there would be a revolution in England sooner than any general acceptance of Conscription; and coming down to more recent events, when the latest huge British war loan provided the only fit and proper answer to German frightfulness at sea.

Let me here say a word on the subject of colonial policy, on which I may perhaps be allowed to speak with a certain amount of authority after extended travel in the farthest corners of Africa, and from an intimate, personal knowledge of German as well as English and French colonies. Germany has less colonial territory than the older colonists, it is true. It is also true that the German struggle for the most widespread, the most intensive and lucrative employment of the energies and capabilities of our highly developed commercial land is justified. But at the risk of being dubbed as absolutely lacking in patriotism, I should like to point out that in the first place the resources we had at our disposal in our own colonial territory in tropical and subtropical Africa, little exploited as they then were, would have amply sufficed for our commercial needs and colonising capacities — though possibly not for our aspirations after world power! And secondly, the very liberal character of England's trade and colonial policy did not hinder us in any way from reaching the top of the commercial tree even in foreign colonies.

Anyone who knows English colonies knows that the British Government, wherever it has been possible to do so politically, that is, in all her colonies which are already properly organised and firmly established as British, has always met in a most generous and sympathetic way German, and indeed any foreign, trade or other enterprises. New firms, with German capital, were received with open arms, their excellence and value for the young country heartily recognised and ungrudgingly encouraged; not the slightest shadow of any jealousy of foreign undertakings could ever exist in a British colony, and every German could be as sure as an Englishman himself of being justly treated in every way and encouraged in the most generous fashion in his work.

2

Thousands of Germans otherwise thoroughly embued with the national spirit make no secret of the fact that they would far rather live in a British than a German colony. Too often in the latter the newcomer was met at every point by an exaggerated bureaucracy and made to feel by some official that he was not a reserve officer, and consequently a social inferior. Hints were dropped to discourage him, and inquiries were even made as to whether he had enough money to book his passage back to where he came from!

Far be it from me to wish to depreciate by these words the value of our own colonial efforts. As pioneers in Africa we were working on the very best possible lines, but we should have been content to go on learning from the much superior British colonial methods, and should have finished and perfected our own domain instead of always shouting jealously about other people's. I am quite convinced that another ten years of undisturbed peaceful competition and Germany, with her own very considerable colonial possessions on the one hand, and the possibility on the other of pushing commercial enterprise on the highest scale not only in independent overseas states but under the beneficent protection of English rule with its true freedom and real furtherance of trade "uplift," would have reached her goal much better than by means of all the sword-rattling Weltpolitik of the Pan-Germans.

It is true that in territory not yet properly organised or guaranteed, politically still doubtful, and in quite new protectorates, especially along the routes to India, where vital English interests are at stake, and on the much-talked-of Persian Gulf, England could not, until her main object was firmly secured, meet in the same fair way German desires with regard to commercial activity. And there she has more than once learnt to her cost the true character of the German Weltpolitik.

That is the real meaning, at any rate so far as colonial politics are concerned, of the German-English contest for a "place in the sun."

3

No one who understands it aright could ever condone the outgrowths of our Weltpolitik, however much he might desire to assist German ability to find practical outlet in all suitable overseas territory, nor could he ever forget the wealth of wonderful deeds, wrought in the service of human civilisation and freedom, Englishmen can place to their credit years before we ever began. With such considerations of justice in view, we should have recognised that there was a limit to our efforts after expansion, and as a matter of fact we should have gone further and fared better—in a decade we should have probably been really wealthy —for the English in their open-handed way certainly left us a surprising amount of room for the free exercise of our commercial talents.

I have intentionally given an illustration only of the colonial side of the problem affecting German-English relations, so that I may avoid dealing with any subject I do not know from personal observation.

It was this English people, that, in spite of all their egoism, have really done something for civilisation, that the German of August 1914 accused of being nothing but a nation of shopkeepers with a cowardly, narrow-minded policy that was unprepared to make any sacrifice for others. It was this people that the German of August 1914—and his spokesman von Bethmann-Hollweg, who later thought it necessary to defend himself against the charge of "having brought too much ethics into politics"—expected to stand by and see Belgium overridden. It was this same England that we believed would hold back even when the Chancellor found it impossible to apply to French colonial possessions the guarantee he had given not to aim at any territorial conquests in the war with France!

And so it was with all the more grimness, with all the more gravity, that on that memorable night of August 4th the terrible blow fell. The English declaration of war entered into the very soul of the German people, who stood as a sacrifice to a political miscalculation that had its roots less in a lack of thought and experience than in a boundless arrogance.

4

About the same time I was a witness of those laughable scenes which took place on the Potsdamer Platz in Berlin, where, in complete misjudgment of the whole political situation Japanese were carried shoulder high by the enthusiastic and worthy citizens of Berlin under the erroneous impression that these obvious archenemies of Russia would naturally be allies of Germany. Every German that was not blind to the trend of true "world-politics" must surely have shaken his head over this lamentable spectacle. A few days afterwards Japan sent its ultimatum against Kiao-Tchao!

It was the same incapability of thinking in terms of true world-politics that led us lately to believe that we might find supporters in Mexico and Japan of the piracy we indulged in as a result of America's intervention in the war, the same incapability that blinded us to the effect our methods must have on other neutrals such as China and the South American States. And although one admits the possibility of a miscalculation being made, yet a miscalculation with regard to England's attitude was not only the height of political stupidity, but showed an absence of moral sense. The moment England entered the war, Germany lost the war.

And while the world-politicians of Berlin, having recovered from their first dismay, were making jokes about the "nation of shopkeepers" and its little army which they would just "have arrested"; while a little later the military events up to St. Quentin and the Battle of the Marne seemed to justify the idle mockers who knew nothing of England and had never even ventured their noses out of Germany,—those who had lived in the colonies were uttering warnings against any kind of optimism, and some already felt the war would end badly for us.

I belonged to the latter group. I expressed my conviction in this direction as early as August 6th, 1914, in a letter which I wrote from Berlin for my father's birthday. In it I maintained that in spite of all our brilliant military successes, which would certainly not last, this war was a mistake and would assuredly end in failure for

Germany. Littera scripta manet. Never from that moment have I believed in final victory for Germany. Slowly but surely then I veered round to the position that I could no longer even desire victory for Germany.

Naturally I did my military duty. I saw the fearful crime Germany was committing, yet I hurried to the front with the millions who believed that Germany was innocent and had been attacked without cause. There was nothing else to be done, and it must of course be remembered that my final rupture with Germany did not take place all of a sudden. After a few months of war in Masuria I was released as unfit for active service as the result of a severe illness.

Of all the many episodes of my life at the front, none is so deeply impressed on my memory as the silent war of mutual hatred I waged with my immediately superior officer, a true prototype of his race, a true Prussian. I can still see him, a man of fifty-five or so, who, in spite of former active service, had only reached the rank of lieutenant, and who, as he told me himself right at the beginning, in very misplaced confidence, rushed into active service again because in this way he could get really good pay and would even have a prospect of further promotion.

This Lieutenant Stein told me too of the first weeks in Belgium, when he had been in command of a company, and I can still hear him boasting about his warlike propensities, and how his teacher had said about him when he was a boy "he was capable of stealing an altar-cloth and cutting it up to make breeches for himself."

"When we wanted to do any commandeering or to plunder a house," so he told me, "there was a very simple means. A man belonging to my company would be ordered to throw a Belgian rifle through an open cellar window, the house would then be searched for weapons, and even if we found only one rifle we had orders to seize everything without mercy and to drive out the occupiers." I can still see the creature standing in front of me and relating this and many a similar tale in these first days before he knew me. I have never forgotten it; and I think I owe much to Lieutenant Stein. He helped me on the way I was predestined to go, for had I not just returned from the colonies and foreign lands, imbued with liberal ideas, and from the first torn by grave doubts?

The Lieutenant may be an exception— granted; but he is an exception unfortunately but too often represented in that army of millions on its invading march into unhappy Belgium, among officers and non-commissioned officers, whom, at any rate so far as active service is concerned, everyone who has served in the German Army will agree with me in calling on the average thoroughly brutal. Lieutenant Stein gave me my first real deep disgust of war. He is a type that I have not invented, and he will easily be identified by the German military authorities from his signature on my military pass as one of those arch-Prussians who suddenly readopt a martial air, suddenly revive and come into their element again, although they may be sickly old valetudinarians—the kind of men who in civil life are probably enthusiastic members of the "German Colonial Society," the "Naval Union," and the "Pan-German Association," and ardent world-politicians of the ale-bench type.

I found his stories afterwards confirmed to the letter by one of the most famous German war-correspondents, Paul Schweder, the author of the four-volume work entitled At Imperial Headquarters. With a naïveté equal to Lieutenant Stein's, and trusting no doubt to my then official position as correspondent of a German paper, he gave me descriptions of Belgian atrocities committed by our soldiers and the results of our system of occupation that, in all their horrible nakedness, put everything that ever appeared in the Entente newspapers absolutely in the shade.

As early as the beginning of 1916 he told me the plain truth that we were practically starving Belgium and that the country was really only kept alive by the Relief Commission, and that we were attempting to ruin any Belgian industry which might compete with ours by a systematic removal of machinery to Germany. And that was before the time of the Deportations!

Schweder's descriptions dealt for the most part with the sexual morality of our soldiers in the trenches. In spite of severe punishments, so he assured me, thousands and thousands of cases occurred of women and young girls out of decent Belgian and French families being outraged. The soldier on short leave from the front, with the prospect of a speedy return to the first-line trenches and death staring him in the face, did not care what happened; the unhappy victims were for the most part silent about their shame, so that the cases of punishment were very few and far between.

While I was at the front I heard extraordinary things, for which I had again detailed confirmation from Schweder, who knew the whole of the Western Front well, about the German policy of persecution in Alsace-Lorraine.

There the system was to punish with imprisonment not only actions but opinions. The authorities did not even scruple to imprison girls out of highly-respected houses who had perhaps made some harmless remark in youthful ignorance, and shut them up with common criminals and prostitutes to work out their long sentence. Such scandalous acts, which are a disgrace to humanity, Paul Schweder confirmed by the dozen or related at first-hand.

He was intelligent enough, too, as was evident from the many statements made by him in confidential circles, to see through the utter lack of foundation, the mendacity, the immorality of what he wrote in his books merely for the sake of filthy lucre; but when I tried one day to take on a bet with him that Verdun would not fall, he took his revenge by spreading the report in Constantinople that I was an Pro-Entente, and doing his utmost to intrigue against me. That is the German war-correspondent's idea of morality!

When I was released from the army in the beginning of 1915, I joined the editorial staff of the Kölnische Zeitung and remained for some weeks in Cologne. I have not retained any very special impressions of this period of my activity, except perhaps the recollection of the spirit of jingoistic Prussianism that I— being a Badener—had scarcely ever come across before in its full glory, and, from the many confidential communications and discussions among the editorial staff, the feeling that even then there was a certain nervousness and insecurity among those who, in their leading articles, informed the public daily of their absolute confidence in victory.

One curious thing at this time, perhaps worthy of mention, was the disdainful contempt with which these Prussians—even before the fall of Przemysl—regarded Austria. But the scornful and biting commentaries made behind the scenes in the editorial sanctum at the fall of this stronghold stood in most striking contrast to what the papers wrote about it.

Later, when I had already been a long time in Turkey, a humorous incident gave me renewed opportunity of seeing this Prussian spirit of unbounded exaggeration of self and depreciation of others. The incident is at the same time characteristic of the spirit of militarism with which the representatives of the German Press are thoroughly imbued, in spite of the opportunities most of them have had through long visits to other countries of gaining a little more savoir faire.

One beautiful summer afternoon at a promenade concert in the "Petit Champs" at Pera I introduced an Austrian Lieutenant of Dragoons I knew, belonging to one of the best regiments, to our Balkan correspondent who happened to be staying in Constantinople: "Lieutenant N.; Herr von M." The correspondent sat down at the table and repeated very distinctly: "Lieutenant-Colonel von M. It turned out that he had been a second lieutenant in the Prussian Army, and had pushed himself up to this wonderful rank in the Bulgarian Army, instinctively combining journalism and militarism. My companion, however, with true Austrian calm, took not the slightest notice of the correction, did not spring up and greet him with an enthusiastic "Ah! my dear fellow-officer, etc.," but began an ordinary social conversation.

Would anyone believe that next day old Herr von M. took me roundly to task for sitting at the same table as an Austrian officer and appearing in public with him, and informed me quasi-officially that as a representative of the Kölnische Zeitung I should associate only with the German colony in Constantinople.

I wonder which is the most irritating characteristic of this type of mind—its overbearing attitude towards our Allies, its jingoistic "Imperial German" cant, or its wounded dignity as a militarist who forgets that he is a journalist and no longer an officer?

CHAPTER II

In Constantinople—Pro-Turkish considerations—The dilemma of a Gallipoli correspondent—Under German military control.

A few days after the fall of Przemysl I set out for Constantinople. I left Germany with a good deal of friendly feeling towards the Turk. I was even quite well disposed towards the Young Turks, although I knew and appreciated the harm caused by their régime and the reproaches levelled against it since 1909. At any rate, when I landed on Turkish soil I was certainly not lacking in goodwill towards the Government of Enver and Talaat, and nothing was further from my thoughts than to prejudice myself against my new sphere of work by any preconceived criticism. In comparison with Abdul-Hamid I regarded the régime of the Young Turks, in spite of all, as a big step in advance and a necessary one, and the parting words of one of our old editors, a thorough connoisseur of Turkey, lingered in my ears without very much effect. He said: "You are going to Constantinople. You will soon be able to see for yourself the moral bankruptcy of the Young Turks, and you will find that Turkey is nothing but a dead body galvanised into action, that will only last as long as the war lasts and we Germans supply the galvanising power." I would not believe it, and went to Turkey with an absolutely open mind to form my own opinion.

It must also be remembered that all the pro-Turkish utterances of Eastern experts of all shades and nationalities who emphasised the fact that the Turks were the most respectable nation of the East, were not without their effect upon me; also I had read Pierre Loti. I was determined to extend to the Turkish Government the strong sympathy I already felt for the Turkish people—and, let me here emphasise it, still feel. To undermine that sympathy, to make me lose my confidence in this race, things would have to go badly indeed. They went worse than I ever thought was possible.

I went first of all to the new Turkish front in the Dardanelles and the Gallipoli Peninsula, where everything was ruled by militarism and there was but little opportunity to worry about politics. The combined attack by sea and land had just begun, and I passed the next few weeks on the Ariburnu front. I found myself in the entirely new position of war-correspondent. I had now to write professionally about this war, which I detested with all my heart and soul.

Well, I simply had to make the back fit the burden. Whatever I did or did not do, I have certainly the clear satisfaction of knowing that I never wrote a single word in praise of war. One will understand that, in spite of my inward conviction that Germany by unloosing the war on Europe had committed a terrible crime against humanity, in spite of my consciousness of acting in a wrong cause, in spite of my deep disgust of much that I had already seen, I was still interested in Turkey's fight for existence, but from quite another standpoint.

As an objective onlooker I did not have to be an absolute hypocrite to do justice to my journalistic duties to my paper. I got to know the Turkish soldier with his stoical heroism in defence, and the brilliant attacking powers and courage of the Anatolians with their blind belief in their Padishah, as they were rushed to the defence of Stamboul and hurled themselves in a bayonet charge against the British machine-guns under a hail of shells from the sea. I gained a high opinion of Turkish valour and powers of resistance. I had no reason to stint my praise or withhold my judgment. In mess-tents and at various observation-posts I made the personal acquaintance of crowds of thoroughly sympathetic and likeable Turkish officers. Let me mention but one—Essad Pasha, the defender of Jannina.

I found quite enough material on my two visits to Gallipoli during various phases of the fighting to write a series of feuilletons without any glorification of militarism and political aims. I confined myself to what was of general human interest, to what was picturesque, what was dramatic in the struggle going on in this unique theatre of war.

But even then I was beginning to have my own opinion about much that I saw; I was already torn by conflicting doubts. Already I was beginning to ask myself whether my sympathies would not gradually turn more and more definitely to those who were vainly storming these strong Turkish forts from the sea, under a deadly machine-gun fire, for the cause of true civilisation, the cause of liberty, was manifestly on their side.

I had opportunity, too, of making comparisons from the dead and wounded and the few prisoners there were between the value of the human material sacrificed on either side—on the one, brave but stupid Anatolians, accustomed to dirt and misery; on the other cultured and highly civilised men, sportsmen from the colonies who had hurried from the farthest corners of the earth to fight not only for the British cause, but for the cause of civilisation. But at that time I was not yet ripe for the decision forced upon me later by other things that I saw with my own eyes; I had not yet reached that deep inward conviction that I should have to make a break with Germany. The only thing I could do and felt compelled to do then was to pay my homage not only to Turkish patriotism and Turkish bravery, but to the wonderful courage and fearlessness of death shown by those whom at that time I had, as a German, to regard as my enemies; this I did over and over again in my articles.

I saw, too, the first indications of other things. Traces of the most outspoken jingoism among Turkish officers became gradually apparent, and more than one Turkish commander pointed out to me with ironical emphasis that things went just as smoothly and promptly in his sector, where there was no German officer in charge, as anywhere else.

On my second visit to the Dardanelles, in summer, I heard of considerable quarrels over questions of rank, and there was more than one outbreak of jingoistic arrogance on the part of both Turkish and German subalterns, leading in some cases even to blows and consequent severe punishment for insubordination. The climax was reached in the scandal of supplanting General Weber, commanding the "Southern Group" (Sedd-ul-Bahr) by Vehib Pasha, a grim and fanatical Turk. In this case the Turkish point of view prevailed, for General Liman von Sanders, Commander-in-Chief of the Gallipoli Army, was determined not to lose his post, and agreed slavishly with all that Enver Pasha ordained.

From other fronts, such as the Irak and the "Caucasus" (which was becoming more and more a purely Armenian theatre of war, without losing that chimerical designation in the official reports!), there came even more significant tales; there German and Turkish officers seemed to live still more of a cat-and-dog life than in the Dardanelles. Of course under the iron discipline of both Turks and Germans, these unpleasant occurrences were never allowed to come to such a pass that they would interfere in any way with military operations, but they were of significance as symptoms of a deep distrust of the Germans even in Turkish military circles.

CHAPTER III

The great Armenian persecutions — The system of Talaat and Enver — A denunciation of Germany as a cowardly and conscienceless accomplice.

In spite of all, I returned to Constantinople from my first visit to the Dardanelles with very little diminution of friendly feeling towards the Turks. My first experience when I returned to the capital was the beginning of the Armenian persecutions. And here I may as well say at once that my love for present-day Turkey perished absolutely with this unique example in the history of modern human civilisation of the most appalling bestiality and misguided jingoism. This, more than everything else I saw on the German-Turkish side throughout the war, persuaded me to take up arms against my own people and to adopt the position I now hold. I say "German-Turkish," for I must hold the German Government as equally responsible with the Turks for the atrocities they allowed them to commit.

Here in neutral Switzerland, where so many of these unfortunate Armenians have taken refuge and such abundance of information is available, so much material has been collected that it is unnecessary for me to go into details in this book. Suffice it to say that the narration of all the heart-rending occurrences that came to my personal knowledge during my stay in Turkey, without my even trying to collect systematic information on the subject, would fill a book. To my deep sorrow I have to admit that, from everything I have heard from reliable sources — from German Red Cross doctors, officials and employees of the Baghdad Railway, members of the American Embassy, and Turks themselves — although they are but individual cases — I cannot regard as exaggerated such appalling facts and reports as are contained for example in Arnold Toynbee's Armenian Atrocities. [1]

In this little book, however, which partakes more of the nature of an essay than an exhaustive treatise, my task will be rather to determine the system, the underlying political thought and the responsibility of Germany in all these horrors—massacres, the seduction of women, children left to die or thrown into the sea, pretty young girls carried off into houses of ill repute, the compulsory conversion to Islam and incorporation in Turkish harems of young women, the ejection from their homes of eminent and distinguished families by brutal gendarmes, attacks while on the march by paid bands of robbers and criminals, "emigration" to notorious malaria swamps and barren desert and mountain lands, victims handed over to the wild lusts of roaming Bedouins and Kurds—in a word, the triumph of the basest brutality and most cold-blooded refinement of cruelty in a war of extermination in which half a million men, and according to some estimates many more, have perished, while the remaining one and a half million of this most intelligent and cultured race, one of the principal pioneers of progress in the Ottoman Empire, see nothing but complete extinction staring them in the face through the rupture of family ties, the deprivation of their rights, and economic ruin.

The Armenian persecutions began in all their cruelty, practically unannounced, in April 1915. Certain events on the Caucasus front, which no number of lies could explain away, gave the Turkish Government the welcome pretext for falling like wild animals on the Armenians of the eastern vilajets—the so-called Armenia Proper—and getting to work there without deference to man, woman, or child. This was called "the restoration of order in the war zone by military measures, rendered necessary by the connivance of the inhabitants with the enemy, treachery and armed

---

[1] This and other works on the subject came to my notice for the first time a few days before going to press. Before that (in Turkey, Austria, and Germany) they were quite unprocurable.

16

support." The first two or three hundred thousand Armenians fell in the first rounding up.

That in those outlying districts situated directly on the Russian frontier a number of Armenians threw in their lot with the advancing Russians, no one will seek to deny, and not a single Armenian I have spoken to denies it. But the "Armenian Volunteer Corps" that fought on the side of Russia was composed for the most part—that at least has been proved beyond doubt—of Russian Armenians settled in Transcaucasian territory.

So far as the Turkish Armenians taking part are concerned, no reasonable being would think of denying Turkey as Sovereign State the formal right of taking stringent measure against these traitors and deserters. But if I expressly recognise this right, I do so with the big reservation that the frightful sufferings undergone for centuries by a people left by their rulers to the mercy of marauding Kurds and oppressed by a government of shameless extortioners, absolutely absolve these deserters in the eyes of the whole civilised world from any moral crime.

And yet I would willingly have gone so far for the benefit of the Turks, in spite of their terrible guilt towards this people, as perhaps to keep my own counsel on the subject, if it had merely been a case of the execution of some hundreds under martial law or the carrying out of other measures—such as deportation—against a couple of thousand Armenians and these strictly confined to men. It is even possible that Europe and America would have pardoned Turkey for taking even stronger steps in the nature of reprisals or measures of precaution against the male inhabitants of that part of Armenia Proper which was gradually becoming a war zone. But from the very beginning the persecutions were carried on against women and children as well as men, were extended to the hundred thousand inhabitants of the six eastern vilajets, and were characterised by such savage brutality that the methods of the slave-drivers of the African interior and the persecution of

17

Christians under Nero are the only thing that can be compared with them.

Every shred of justification for the Turkish Government in their attempt to establish this as an "evacuation necessary for military purposes and for the prevention of unrest" entirely vanishes in face of such methods, and I do not believe that there is a single decent German, cognisant of the facts of the case, who is not filled with real disgust of the Young Turkish Government by such cold-blooded butchery of the inhabitants of whole districts and the deportation of others with the express purpose of letting them die en route. Anyone with human feelings, however pro-Turkish he may be politically, cannot think otherwise.

This "evacuation necessary for military purposes" emptied Armenia Proper of men. How often have Turks themselves told me—I could mention names, but I will not expose my informants, who were on the whole decent exceptions to the rule, to the wrath of Enver or Talaat—how often have they assured me that practically not a single Armenian is to be found in Armenia! And it is equally certain that scarcely one can be left alive of all that horde of deported men who escaped the first massacres and were hunted up hill and down dale in a state of starvation, exposed to attacks by Kurds, decimated by spotted typhus, and finally abandoned to their fate in the scorching deserts of Northern Mesopotamia and Northern Syria. One has only to read the statistics of the population of the six vilajets of Armenia Proper to discover the hundreds of thousands of victims of this wholesale murder.

But unfortunately that was not all. The Turkish Government went farther, much farther. They aimed at the whole Armenian people, not only in Armenia itself, but also in the "Diaspora," in Anatolia Proper and in the capital. They were at that time some hundred thousand. In this case they could scarcely go on the principle of "evacuation of the war zone," for the inhabitants were hundreds of

18

miles both from the Eastern front and from the Dardanelles, so they had to resort to other measures.

They suddenly and miraculously discovered a universal conspiracy among the Armenians of the Empire. It was only by a trick of this kind that they could succeed in carrying out their system of exterminating the entire Armenian race. The Turkish Government skilfully influenced public opinion throughout the whole world, and then discovered, nay, arranged for, local conspiracies. They then falsified all the details so that they might go on for months in peace and quiet with their campaign of extermination.

In a series of semi-official articles in the newspapers of the Committee of Young Turks it was made quite clear that all Armenians were dangerous conspirators who, in order to shake off the Ottoman yoke, had collected firearms and bombs and had arranged, with the help of English and Russian money, for a terrible slaughter of Turks on the day that the English fleet overcame the armies on the Dardanelles.

I must here emphasise the fact that all the arguments the Turkish Government brought against the Armenians did not escape my notice. They were indeed evident enough in official and semi-official publications and in the writings of German "experts on Turkey." I investigated everything, even right at the beginning of my stay in Turkey, and always from a thoroughly pro-Turkish point of view. That did not prevent me however, from coming to my present point of view.

Herr Zimmermann, the Secretary of State for Foreign Affairs, has only got to refer to the date of his letter to the editorial staff of my paper, in which he speaks of my confidential report to the paper on this subject which went through his hands and aroused his interest, and he will find what opinions I held as early as the summer of 1916 on the subject of the Armenian persecutions—and this without my having any particular sympathy for the Armenians, for it was not till much later that I got to know them and their high intellectual qualities through personal intercourse.

Here I can only give my final judgment on all these pros and cons, and say to the best of my knowledge and opinion, that after the first act in this drama of massacre and death—the brutal "evacuation of the war zone" in Armenia Proper—the meanest, the lowest, the most cynical, most criminal act of race-fanaticism that the history of mankind has to show was the extension of the system of deportation, with its wilful neglect and starvation of the victims, to further hundreds of thousands of Armenians in the Capital and Interior. And these were people who, through their place of residence, their surroundings, their social status, their preoccupation in work and wage-earning, were quite incapable of taking any active part in politics.

Others of them, again, belonged to families of high social standing and culture, bound to the land by a thousand ties, coming of a well-to-do, old-established stock, and from traditional training and ordinary prudence holding themselves scrupulously apart from all revolutionary doings. All were surrounded by a far superior number of inhabitants belonging to other races.

This diabolical crime was committed solely and only because of the Turkish feeling of economic and intellectual inferiority to that non-Turkish element, for the set purpose of obtaining handsome compensation for themselves, and was undertaken with the cowardly acquiescence of the German Government in full knowledge of the facts.

Of this long chain of crime I saw at least the beginning thousands of times with my own eyes. Hardly had I returned from my first visit to the Dardanelles when these persecutions began in the whole of Anatolia and even in Constantinople, and continued with but slight intermissions of a week or two at different times till shortly before I left Constantinople in December 1916.

That was the time when in the flourishing western vilajets of Anatolia, beginning with Brussa and Adabazar, where the well-stocked farms in Armenian hands must have been an eyesore to a Government that had written "forcible nationalisation" on their standard, the whole household goods of respectable families were thrown into the street and sold for a mere nothing, because their owners often had only an hour till they were routed out by the waiting gendarme and hustled off into the Interior. The fittings of the houses, naturally unsaleable in the hurry, usually fell to the lot of marauding "mohadjis" (Mohammedan immigrants), who, often enough armed to the teeth by the "Committee," began the disturbances which were then exposed as "Armenian conspiracies."

That was the time when mothers, apparently in absolute despair, sold their own children, because they had been robbed of their last penny and could not let their children perish on that terrible march into the distant Interior.

How many countless times did I have to look on at that typical spectacle of little bands of Armenians belonging to the capital being escorted through the streets of Pera by two gendarmes in their ragged murky grey uniforms with their typical brutal Anatolian faces, while a policeman who could read and write marched behind with a notebook in his hand beckoning people at random out of the crowd with an imperious gesture, and if their papers showed them to be Armenians, simply herding them in with the rest and marching them off to the "Karakol" of Galata-Seraï, the chief police-station in Pera, where he delivered up his daily bag of Armenians!

The way these imprisonments and deportations were carried on is a most striking confutation of the claims of the Turkish Government that they were acting only in righteous indignation over the discovery of a great conspiracy. This is entirely untrue.

With the most cold-blooded calculation and method, the number of Armenians to be deported were divided out over a period of many months, indeed one may say over nearly a year and a half. The deportations only began to abate when the downfall of the Armenian Patriarchate in summer 1916 dealt the final blow to the social life of the Armenians. They more or less ceased in December 1916 with the gathering-in of all those who had formerly paid the military exemption tax —among them many eminent Armenian business men.

What can be said of the "righteous, spontaneous indignation" of the Armenian Government when, for example, of two Armenian porters belonging to the same house—brothers —one is deported to-day and the other not till a fortnight later; or when the number of Armenians to be delivered up daily from a certain quarter of the town is fixed at a definite figure, say two hundred or a thousand, as I have been told was the case by reliable Turks who were in full touch with the police organisation and knew the system of these deportations?

Of the ebb and flow of these persecutions, all that can be said is that the daily number of deportations increased when the Turks were annoyed over some Russian victory, and that the banishments miraculously abated when the military catastrophes of Erzerum, Trebizond, and Erzindjan gave the Government food for thought and led them to wonder if perhaps Nemesis was going to overtake them after all.

And then the method of transport! Every day towards evening, when these unfortunate creatures had been collected in the police-stations, the women and children were packed into electric-trams while the men and boys were compelled to go off on foot to Galata with a couple of blankets and only the barest necessities for their terrible journey packed in a small bag. Of course they were not all poor people by any means.

This dire fate might befall anyone any day or any hour, from the caretaker and the tradesman to members of the best families. I know cases where men of high education, belonging to aristocratic families—engineers, doctors, lawyers—were banished from Pera in this disgusting way under cover of darkness to spend the night on the platforms of the Haidar-Pasha station, and then be packed off in the morning on the Anatolian Railway—of course they paid for their tickets and all travelling expenses!—to the Interior, where they died of spotted typhus, or, in rare cases after their recovery from this terrible malady, were permitted, after endless pleading, to return broken in body and soul to their homes as "harmless." Among these bands herded about from pillar to post like cattle there were hundreds and thousands of gentle, refined women of good family and of perfect European culture and manners.

For the most part it was the sad fate of those deported to be sent off on an endless journey by foot, to the far-off Arabian frontier, where they were treated with the most terrible brutality. There, in the midst of a population wholly foreign and but little sympathetic to their race, left to their fate on a barren mountain-side, without money, without shelter, without medical assistance, without the means of earning a livelihood, they perished in want and misery.

The women and children were always separated from the men. That was the characteristic of all the deportations. It was an attempt to strike at the very core of their national being and annihilate them by the tearing asunder of all family ties.

That was how a very large part of the Armenian people disappeared. They were the "persons transported elsewhere," as the elegant title of the "Provisional Han" ran, which gave full stewardship over their well-stocked farms to the "Committee" with its zeal for "internal colonisation" with purely Turkish elements. In this way the great goal was reached—the forcible nationalisation of a land of mixed races.

While Anatolia was gradually emptied of all the forces that had hitherto made for progress, while the deserted towns and villages and flourishing fields of those who had been banished fell into the hands of the lowest "Mohadjr"—hordes of the most dissipated Mohammedan emigrants—that stream of unhappy beings trickled on ever more slowly to its distant goal, leaving the dead bodies of women and children, old men and boys, as milestones to mark the way. The few that did reach the "settlement" alive—that is, the fever-ridden, hunger-stricken concentration camps—continually molested by raiding Bedouins and Kurds, gradually sickened and died a slower and even more terrible death.

Sometimes even this was not speedy enough for the Government, and a case occurred in Autumn 1916—absolutely verified by statements made by German employees on the Baghdad Railway— where some thousands of Armenians, brought as workers to this stretch of railway, simply vanished one day without leaving a trace. Apparently they were simply shipped off into the desert without more ado and there massacred.

This terrible catalogue of crime on the part of the Government of Talaat is, however, in spite of all censorship and obstruction, being dealt with officially in all quarters of the globe —by the American Embassy at Constantinople and in neutral and Entente countries— and at the conclusion of peace it will be brought as an accusation against the criminal brotherhood of Young Turks by a merciless court of all the civilised nations of the world.

I have spoken to Armenians who have said to me, "In former times the old Sultan Abdul-Hamid used to have us massacred by thousands. We were delivered over by well-organised pogroms to the Kurds at stated times, and certainly we suffered cruelly enough. Then the Young Turks, as Adana 1909 shows, started on a bloodshed of thousands. But after what we have just gone through we long with all our hearts for the days of the old massacres. Now it is no longer a case of a certain number of massacred; now our whole people is being slowly but surely exterminated by the national hatred of an apparently civilised, apparently modern, and therefore infinitely more dangerous Government.

"Now they get hold of our women and children and send them long journeys on foot to concentration camps in barren districts where they die. The pitiful remains of our population in the villages and towns of the Interior, where the local authorities have carried out the commands of the central Government most zealously, are forcibly converted to Islam, and our young girls are confined in Turkish harems and places of low repute.

"The race is to vanish to the very last man, and why? Because the Turks have recognised their intellectual bankruptcy, their economic incompetence, and their social inferiority to the progressive Armenian element, to which Abdul-Hamid, in spite of occasional massacres, knew well enough how to adapt himself, and which he even utilised in all its power in high offices of state. Because now that they themselves are being decimated by a weary and unsuccessful war of terrible bloodshed that was lost before it was begun, they hope in this way to retain the sympathy of their peoples and preserve the superiority of their element in the State.

"These are not sporadic outbursts of wrath, as they were in the case of Hamid, but a definitely thought-out political measure against our people, and for this very reason they can hope for no mercy. Germany, as we have seen, tolerates the annihilation of our people through weakness and lack of conscience, and if the war lasts much longer the Armenian people will have ceased to exist. That is why we long for the old régime of Abdul-Hamid, terrible as it was for us."

Has there ever been a greater tragedy in the history of a people— and of a people that have never held any illusions as to political independence, wedged in as they are between two Great Powers, and who had no real irredentistic feelings towards Russia, and, up to the moment when the Young Turks betrayed them shamefully and broke the ties of comradeship that had bound them together as revolutionaries against the old despotic system of Abdul-Hamid, were as thoroughly loyal citizens of the Ottoman Empire as any of the other peoples of this land, excepting perhaps the Turks themselves.

I hope that these few words may have given sufficient indication of the spirit and outcome of this system of extermination. I should like to mention just one more episode which affected me personally more than anything I experienced in Turkey.

One day in the summer of 1916 my wife went out alone about midday to buy something in the "Grand Rue de Péra." We lived a few steps from Galata-Seraï and had plenty of opportunity from our balcony of seeing the bands of Armenian deportees arriving at the police-station under the escort of gendarmes. Familiarity with such sights finally dulled our sympathies, and we began to think of them not as episodes affecting human individuals, but rather as political events.

On this particular day, however, my wife came back to the house trembling all over. She had not been able to go on her errand. As she passed the "karakol," she had heard through the open hall door the agonising groans of a tortured being, a dull wailing like the sound of an animal being tormented to death. "An Armenian," she was informed by the people standing at the door. The crowd was then dispersed by a policeman.

"If such scenes occur in broad daylight in the busiest part of the European town of Pera, I should like to know what is done to Armenians in the uncivilised Interior," my wife asked me. "If the Turks act like wild beasts here in the capital, so that a woman going through the main streets gets a shock like that to her nerves, then I can't live in this frightful country." And then she burst into a fit of sobbing and let loose all her pent-up passion against what she and I had had to witness for more than a year every time we set a foot out of doors.

"You are brutes, you Germans, miserable brutes, that you tolerate this from the Turks when you still have the country absolutely in your hands. You are cowardly brutes, and I will never set foot in your horrible country again. God, how I hate Germany!"

It was then, when my own wife, trembling and sobbing, in grief, rage, and disgust at such cowardliness, flung this denunciation of my country in my teeth that I finally and absolutely broke with Germany. Unfortunately I had known only too long that it had to come.

I thought of the conversations I had had about the Armenian question with members of the German Embassy in Constantinople and, of a very different kind, with Mr. Morgenthau, the American Ambassador.

I had never felt fully convinced by the protestations of the German Embassy that they had done their utmost to put a check on the murderous attacks on harmless Armenians far from the theatre of war, who from their whole surroundings and their social class could not be in a position to take an active part in politics, and on the cold-blooded neglect and starvation of women and children apparently deported for no other reason than to die. The attitude of the German Government towards the Armenian question had impressed me as a mixture of cowardice and lack of conscience on the one hand and the most short-sighted stupidity on the other.

The American Ambassador, who took the most generous interest in the Armenians, and has done so much for the cause of humanity in Turkey, was naturally much too reserved on this most burning question to give a German journalist like myself his true opinion about the attitude of his German colleagues. But from the many conversations and discussions I had with him, I gathered nothing that would turn me from the opinion I had already formed of the German Embassy, and I had given him several hints of what that opinion was.

The attitude of Germany was, in the first place, as I have said, one of boundless cowardice. For we had the Turkish Government firmly enough in hand, from the military as well as the financial and political point of view, to insist upon the observance of the simplest principles of humanity if we wanted to. Enver, and still more Talaat, who as Minister of the Interior and really Dictator of Turkey was principally responsible for the Armenian persecutions, had no other choice than to follow Germany's lead unconditionally, and they would have accepted without any hesitation, if perhaps with a little grumbling, any definite ruling of Germany's even on this Armenian question that lay so near their hearts.

From hundreds of examples it has been proved that the Germany Embassy never showed any undue delicacy for even perfectly legitimate Turkish interests and feelings in matters affecting German interests, and that they always got their own way where it was a question, for example, of Germans being oppressed, or superseded by Turks in the Government and ruling bodies. And yet I had to stand and look on when our Embassy was not even capable of granting her due and proper rights to a perfectly innocent German lady married to an Armenian who had been deported with many other Armenians. She appealed for redress to the German Embassy, but her only reward was to wait day after day in the vestibule of the Embassy for her case to be heard.

Turks themselves have found cynical enjoyment in this measureless cowardice of ours and compared it with the attitude of the Russian Government, who, if they had found themselves in a similar position to Germany, would have been prepared, in spite of the Capitulations being abolished, to make a political case, if necessary, out of the protection due to one poor Russian Jew. Turks have, very politely but none the less definitely, made it quite clear to me that at bottom they felt nothing but contempt for our policy of letting things slide.

Our attitude was characterised, secondly, by lack of conscience. To look on while life and property, the well-being and culture of thousands, are sacrificed, and to content oneself with weak formal protests when one is in a position to take most energetic command of the situation, is nothing but the most criminal lack of conscience, and I cannot get rid of the suspicion that, in spite of the fine official phrases one was so often treated to in the German Embassy on the subject of the "Armenian problem," our diplomats were very little concerned with the preservation of this people.

What leads me to bring this terrible charge against them? The fact that I never saw anything in all this pother on the part of our diplomats when the venerable old Armenian Patriarch appeared at the Embassy with his suite after some particularly frightful sufferings of the Armenian population, and begged with tears in his eyes for help from the Embassy, however late—and I assisted more than once at such scenes in the Embassy and listened to the conversations of the officials—I never saw anything but concern about German prestige and offended vanity. As far as I saw, there was never any concern for the fate of the Armenian people. The fact that time and again I heard from the mouths of Germans of all grades, from the highest to the lowest, so far as they did not have to keep strictly to the official German versions, expressions of hatred against the Armenians which were based on the most short-sighted judgment, had no relation to the facts of the case, and were merely thoughtless echoes of the official Turkish statements.

And cases have actually been proved to have occurred, from the testimony of German doctors and Red Cross nurses returned from the Interior, of German officers light-heartedly taking the initiative in exterminating and scattering the Armenians when the less-zealous local authorities who still retained some remnants of human feeling, scrupled to obey the instructions of "Nur-el-Osmanieh" (the headquarters of the Committee at Stamboul).

The case is well known and has been absolutely verified of the scandalous conduct of two German officers passing through a village in far Asia Minor, where the Armenians had taken refuge in their houses and barricaded them to prevent being herded off like cattle.

The order had been given that guns were to be turned on them, but not a single Turk had the courage to carry out this order and fire on women and children. Without any authority whatsoever, the two German officers then turned to and gave an exhibition of their shooting capacities!

Such shameful acts are of course isolated cases, but they are on a par with the opinions expressed about the Armenian people by dozens of educated Germans of high position -not to speak of military men at all.

A case of this kind where German soldiers were guilty of an attack on Armenians in the interior of Anatolia, was the subject of frequent official discussion at the German Embassy, and was finally brought to the notice of the authorities in Germany by Graf Wolff-Metternich, a really high-principled and humane man. The material result of this was that through the unheard-of cowardice of our Government, this man -who in spite of his age and in contrast to the weak-minded Freiherr von Wangenheim, and criminally optimistic had made many an attempt to get a firmer grip of the Turkish Government was simply hounded out of office by the Turks and weakly sacrificed without a struggle by Berlin.

What, finally, is one to think of the spirit of our German officials in regard to the Armenian question, when one hears such well-verified tales as were told me shortly before I left Constantinople by an eminent Hungarian banker (whose name I will not reveal) ? He related, for example, that "a German officer, with the title of Baron, and closely connected with the military attaché," went one day to the bazaar in Stamboul and chose a valuable carpet from an Armenian, which he had put down to his account and sent to his house in Pera. Then when it came to paying for it, he promptly set the price twenty pounds lower than had been stipulated, and indicated to the Armenian dealer that in view of the good understanding between himself (the officer) and the Turkish President of police, he would do well not to trouble him further in the matter! I only cite this case because I am unfortunately compelled to believe in its absolute authenticity.

Shortsighted stupidity, finally, is how I characterised the inactive toleration on the part of our Imperial representatives of this policy of extermination of the Armenian race. Our Government could not have been blind to the breaking flood of Turkish jingoism, and no one with any glimmer of foresight could have doubted for a moment since the summer of 1915 that Turkey would only go with us so long as she needed our military and financial aid, and that we should have no place, not even a purely commercial one, in a fully turkified Turkey.

In spite of the lamentations one heard often enough from the mouths of officials over this well-recognised and unpalatable fact, we tolerated the extermination of a race of over one and a half million of people of progressive culture, with the European point of view, intellectually adaptable, absolutely free from jingoism and fanaticism, and eminently cosmopolitan in feeling; we permitted the disappearance of the only conceivable counterbalance to the hopelessly nationalistic, anti-foreign Young Turkish element, and through our cowardice and lack of conscience have made deadly enemies of the few that will rise from the ruins of a race that used to be in thorough sympathy with Germany.

An intelligent German Government would, in face of the increasingly evident Young Turkish spirit, have used every means in their power to retain the sympathies of the Armenians, and indeed to win them in greater numbers. The Armenians waited for us, trembled with impatience for us, to give a definite ruling. Their disappointment, their hatred of us is unbounded now—and rightly so—and if a German ever again wants to take up business in the East he will have to reckon with this afflicted people so long as one of them exists.

To answer the Armenian question in the way I have done here, one does not necessarily need to have the slightest liking or the least sympathy for them as a race. (I have, however, intimated that they deserve at least that much from their high intellectual and social abilities. One only requires to have a feeling for humanity to abhor the way in which hundreds of thousands of these unfortunate people were disposed of; one only requires to understand the commercial and social needs of a vast country like Turkey, so undeveloped and yet so capable of development, to place the highest value on the preservation of this restless, active, and eminently useful element; one only requires to open one's eyes and look at the facts dispassionately to deny utterly and absolutely what the Turks have tried to make the world believe about the Armenians, in order that they might go on with their work of extermination in peace and quiet; one only requires to have a slight feeling of one's dignity as a German to refuse to condone the pitiful cowardice of our Government over the Armenian question.

The mixture of cowardice, lack of conscience, and lack of foresight of which our Government has been guilty in Armenian affairs is quite enough to undermine completely the political loyalty of any thinking man who has any regard for humanity and civilisation. Every German cannot be expected to bear as light-heartedly as the diplomats of Pera the shame of having history point to the fact that the annihilation, with every refinement of cruelty, of a people of high social development, numbering over one and a half million, was contemporaneous with Germany's greatest power in Turkey.

32

In long confidential reports to my paper I made perfectly clear to them the whole position with regard to the Armenian persecutions and the brutal jingoistic spirit of the Young Turks apparent in them. The Foreign Office, too, took notice of these reports. But I saw no trace of the fruits of this knowledge in the attitude of my paper.

The determination never to re-enter the editorial offices of that paper came to me on that dramatic occasion when my wife hurled her denunciation of Germany in my teeth. I at least owe a personal debt of gratitude to the poor murdered and tortured Armenians, for it is to them I owe my moral and political enfranchisement.

CHAPTER IV

The tide of war—Enver's offensive for the "liberation of the Caucasus"—The Dardanelles Campaign; the fate of Constantinople twice hangs in the balance— Nervous tension in international Pera—Bulgaria's attitude—Turkish rancour against her former enemy—-German illusions of a separate peace with Russia—King Ferdinand's time-serving—Lack of munitions in the Dardanelles—A mysterious death: a political murder?— The evacuation of Gallipoli— The Turkish version of victory— Constantinople unreleased — Kut-el-Amara — Propaganda for the "Holy War"—A prisoner of repute—Loyalty of Anglo-Indian officers—Turkish communiqués and their worth—The fall of Erzerum—Official lies— The treatment of prisoners—Political speculation with prisoners of war— Treatment of enemy subjects—Stagnation and lassitude in the summer of 1916—The Greeks in Turkey—Dread of Greek massacres—Rumania's entry—Terrible disappointment—The three phases of the war for Turkey.

It will be necessary to devote a few lines to a review of the principal features of the war, so far as it affected the life of the Turkish capital, in order to have a military and political background for what I saw among the Turks during my twenty months' stay in their country. To that I will add a short description of the economic situation.

When I arrived in Constantinople, Turkey had already completed her first winter campaign in the Caucasus, and had repelled the attack of the Entente fleet on the Dardanelles, culminating in the events of March 18th, 1915. But Enver Pasha had completely misjudged the relation between the means at his disposal and the task before him when, out of pure vanity and a mad desire for expansion, he undertook a personally conducted offensive for "the liberation of the Caucasus." The terrible defeats inflicted on the Turkish army on this occasion were kept from the knowledge of the people by a rigorous censorship and the falsification of the communiqués. This was particularly the case in the enormous Turkish losses sustained at Sarykamish.

Enver had put this great Caucasus offensive in hand out of pure wanton folly, thinking by so doing to win laurels for himself and to have something tangible to show those Turkish ultra-Nationalists who always had an eye on Turkestan and Turan and thought that now was the time to carry out their programme of a "Greater Turkey." It was this mad undertaking, bound as it was to come to grief, that first showed Enver Pasha in his true colours. I shall have something to say about his character in another connection, which will show how gravely he has been over-estimated in Europe.

From the beginning of March 1915 to the beginning of January 1916 the situation was practically entirely commanded by the battles in the Dardanelles and Gallipoli. It has now been accepted as a recognised fact even in the countries belonging to the Entente that the sacrifice of a few more ships on March 18th would have decided the fate of the Dardanelles. To their great astonishment the gallant defenders of the coast forts found that the attack had suddenly ceased. Dozens of the German naval gunners who were manning the batteries of Chanakkalé on that memorable day told me later that they had quite made up their minds the fleet would ultimately win, and that they themselves could not have held out much longer. Such an outcome was expected hourly in Constantinople, and I was told by influential people that all the archives, stores of money, etc., had already been removed to Konia.

It is a remarkable fact that for a second time, in the first days of September, the fate of Constantinople was again hanging in the balance — a fact which is no longer a secret in England and France. The British had extended their line northwards from Ariburnu to Anaforta, and a heroic dash by the Anzacs had captured the summit of the Koja-Jemen-Dagh, and so given them direct command of the whole peninsula of Gallipoli and the insufficiently protected Dardanelles forts behind them. It is still a mystery to the people of Constantinople why the British troops did not follow up this victory. The fact is that this time again the money and archives were hurried off from Constantinople to Asia, and a German officer in Constantinople gave me the entertaining information that he had really seriously thought of hiring a window in the Grand' Rue de Péra, so that he and his family might watch the triumphal entry of the Entente troops! It would be easier to enjoy the joke of this if it were not overshadowed by such fearful tragedy.

I have already indicated the dilemma in which I was placed on my first and second visits to the Gallipoli front. I was torn by conflicting doubts as to whom my sympathies ought ultimately to turn to—to the heroic Turkish defender, who was indeed fighting for the existence of his country, although in an unsuccessful and unjust cause, for German militarism and the exaggerated jingoism of the Young Turks, or to those who were officially my enemies but whom, knowing as I did who was responsible for the great crime of the war, I could not regard as such.

In those September days I had already had some experience of Turkish politics and their defiance of the laws of humanity, and my sympathies were all for those thousands of fine colonial troops— such men as one seldom sees— sacrificing their lives in one last colossal attack, which if it had been prolonged even for another hour might have sealed the fate of the Straits and would have meant the first decisive step towards the overthrow of our forces; for the capture of Constantinople would have been the beginning of the end. I am not ashamed to confess that, German as I am, that was the only feeling I had when I heard of the British victory and the subsequent British defeat at Anaforta. The Battle of Anaforta was the last desperate attempt to break the resistance in the Dardanelles.

While the men of Stamboul and Anatolia— the nucleus of the Ottoman Empire—were defending the City of the Caliph at the gate of the Dardanelles, with reinforcements from Arab regiments when they were utterly exhausted in the autumn, the other half of the metropolis, the cosmopolitan Galata-Pera, was trembling for the safety of the attacking Entente troops, and lived through the long months in a state of continual tension, longing always for the moment of release.

There was a great deal of nervous calculation about the probable attitude of Bulgaria among both the Turks and the thousands of thoroughly illoyal citizens of the Ottoman Empire composing the population of the capital. From lack of information and also as a result of Bulgaria's long delay in declaring her attitude, an undue optimism ruled right up to the last moment among those who desired the overthrow of the Turks.

The Bulgarian question was closely bound up with the question of the munitions supply. The Turkish resistance on Gallipoli threatened to collapse through lack of munitions, and general interest centred—with very varied desires with regard to the outcome—on the rare ammunition trains that were brought through Rumania only after an enormous expenditure of Turkish powers of persuasion and the application of any amount of "palm-oil."

I was present at Sedd-ul-Bahr at the beginning of July, when, owing to lack of ammunition, the German-Turkish artillery could only reply with one shot to every ten British ones, while the insufficiently equipped factories of Top-hané and Zeitun-burnu, under the control of General Pieper, Director of Munitions, were turning out as many shells as was possible with the inferior material at their disposal, and the Turkish fortresses in the Interior had to send their supply of often very antiquated ammunition to the Dardanelles.

The whole dramatic import of the situation, which might any day give rise to epoch-making events, was only too evident in Constantinople. It is not to be wondered at that everyone looked forward with feverish impatience to Bulgaria's entry either on one side or the other.

But, in spite of all this, the Turks could scarcely bear the sight of the first Bulgarian soldiers who appeared in autumn 1915 in full uniform in the streets of "Carihrad." The necessary surrender of the land along the Maritza right to the gates of the holy city of "Edirne" (Adrianople) was but little to the liking of the Turkish patriots, and even the successful issue of the Dardanelles campaign, only made possible by Bulgaria's joining the Central Powers, was not sufficient to win the real sympathies of the Turks for their new allies. It was not until much later that the position was altered as a result of the combined fighting in Dobrudja. Practically right up to the end of 1916, the real, short-sighted, jingoistic Turk looked askance at his new ally and viewed with irritation and distrust the desecration of his sacred "Edirne," the symbol of his national renaissance, while the ambition of all politicians was to bring Bulgaria one day to a surrender of the lost territory and more.

Even in 1916 I found Young Turks, belonging to the Committee, who still regarded the Bulgarians as their erstwhile cunning foe and as a set of unscrupulous, unsympathetic opportunists who might again become a menace to them. They even admitted that the Serbs were "infinitely nicer enemies in the Balkan war," and appealed to them very much more than the Bulgarians. The late Prince Yussuf Izzedin Effendi, of whose tragic death I shall speak later, was always a declared opponent of the cession of the Maritza territory.

The possibility of Bulgaria's voluntarily surrendering this territory and possibly much more through extending her own possessions westward if Greece joined the Entente, had a great deal to do with Turkey's attitude during the whole of 1916, and goes far to explain why she dallied so long over the idea of alienating Greece, and used all sorts of chicanery against the Ottoman and Hellenic Greeks in Turkey. Another and much more important factor was, as we shall see, fundamental racehatred and avarice.

38

As the question as to which side Bulgaria was to join was of decisive moment for Turkish politics, I may perhaps be permitted to add a few details from personal information. I had an interesting sidelight on the German attempts to win over Bulgaria from a well-informed source in Sofia. Everyone was much puzzled over the apparent clumsiness of the German Ambassador in Sofia, Dr. Michahelles, in his diplomatic mission to gain help from Bulgaria. King Ferdinand, of course, made great difficulties, and at a very early stage of the proceedings he turned to the Prime Minister, Radoslavoff, and said: "Away with your German Jews! Why don't you take the good French gold?" (referring, of course, to the offered French loan).

The king was cunning enough in his own way, but he was a poor politician and utterly vacillating, for he had no sort of ideals to live up to and was prompted by a spirit of unworthy opportunism, and it needed Radoslavoff's threat of instant resignation to bring him to a definite decision. The transference shortly afterwards of the German Ambassador to a northern post strengthened the impression in confidential circles in Sofia that he had been lacking in diplomacy.

The truth was that he had received most contradictory instructions from Berlin, which did not allow him to do his utmost to win Bulgaria for the German cause. The Imperial Chancellor seems even then — it was after the great German summer offensive against Russia — to have given serious consideration to the possibility of a separate peace with Russia, and was quite convinced that Russia would never lay down arms without having humiliated Bulgaria, should the latter prove a traitor to the Slavic cause and turn against Serbia.

In diplomatic circles in Berlin this knowledge and the decision — so naïve in view of all their boasted Weltpolitik — to pursue the quite illusory dream of a separate peace with Russia, seemed to outweigh, at any rate for some time, anxiety with regard to the state of affairs in Gallipoli and the complete lack of munitions shortly to be expected, and lamed their initiative in their dealings with Bulgaria.

It is probably not generally known that here again the military party assumed the lead in politics, and took the Bulgarian matter in hand themselves. In the space of no time at all, Bulgaria's entry on the German side was an accomplished fact. It was Colonel von Leipzig, the German military attaché at the Constantinople Embassy, that clinched the matter at the critical moment by a journey to Sofia, and the whole thing was arranged in less than a fortnight. But that journey cost him his life. On the way back to the Turkish capital Herr von Leipzig—one of the nicest and most gentlemanly men that ever wore a field-grey uniform—visited the Dardanelles front, and on the little Thracian railway-station of Uzunköprü he met his death mysteriously. He was found shot through the head in the bare little waiting-room of this miserable wayside station.

It so happened that on my way to the Dardanelles on that day at the end of June 1915, I passed through this little station, and was the sole European witness of this tragic event, which increased still further the excitement already hanging over Constantinople in these weeks of lack of ammunition and terrible onslaughts against Gallipoli, and which had already risen to fever-heat over the nervous rumours that were going the rounds as to Bulgaria's attitude. The occurrence, of course, was used by political intriguers for their own ends.

I wrote a warm and truly heartfelt appreciation of this excellent man and good friend, which was published in my paper at the time, and it was not till long afterwards, weeks, indeed, after my return, that I had any idea that the sudden death of Herr von Leipzig on his return from a mission of the highest political importance was looked upon by the German anti-English party as the work of English spies in the service of Mr. Fitzmaurice, who was formerly at the English Embassy in Constantinople.

I was an eye-witness of the occurrence, or rather, I was beside the Colonel a minute after I heard the shot, and saw the hole in his revolver-holster where the bullet had gone through. I heard the frank evidence of all the Turks present, from the policeman who had arrived first on the scene to the staff doctor who came later, and I immediately telegraphed to my paper from the scene of the accident, giving them my impression of the affair.

On my return to Constantinople I was invited to give evidence under oath before the German Consulate General, and there one may find the written evidence of what I had to say: a pure and absolute accident.

I must not omit to mention here that the German authorities themselves in Constantinople were so thoroughly convinced that the idea of murder was out of the question, that Colonel von Leipzig's widow, who, believing this version of the story, hurried to Turkey, to make her own investigations, had the greatest difficulty in being officially received by the Embassy and Consulate. I had a long interview with her in the "Pera Palace," where she complained bitterly of her treatment in this respect. I have tarried a little over this tragic episode as it shows all the political ramifications that ran together in the Turkish capital and the dramatic excitement that prevailed.

The day came, however, when the Entente troops first evacuated Anaforta-Ariburnu, and then, after a long and protracted struggle, Sedd-ul-Bahr, and so the entire Gallipoli Peninsula. The Dardanelles campaign was at an end.

The impossibility of ever breaking down that solid Turkish resistance, the sufferings of the soldiers practically starved to death in the trenches during the cold winter storms, the difficulties of

41

obtaining supplies of provisions, drinking water, ammunition, etc., with a frozen sea and harbourless coast, anxiety about the superior heavy artillery that the enemy kept bringing up after the overthrow of Serbia— everything combined to strengthen the Entente in their decision to put an end to the campaign in Gallipoli.

The Turkish soldiers had now free access to the sea, for all the British Dreadnoughts and cruisers had disappeared; the warlike activity which had raged for months on the narrow Gallipoli Peninsula suddenly ceased; Austrian heavy and medium howitzers undertook the coast defence, and a garrison of a few thousand Turkish soldiers stayed behind in the Narrows for precaution's sake, while the whole huge Gallipoli army in an endless train was marched off to the Taurus to meet the Russian advance threatening in Armenia.

But Constantinople remained "unrelieved." And from that moment a dull resignation, a dreary waiting for one scarcely knew what, disappointment, and pessimism took the place of the nervous tension that had been so apparent in those who had been longing for the fall of the Turkish capital.

But the Turks rejoiced. It is scarcely to be wondered at that they tried to construe the failure of the Gallipoli affair as a wonderful and dazzling victory for Islam over the combined forces of the Great Powers. It is only in line of course with Turkish official untruthfulness that, in shameless perversion of facts, they talked glibly of the irresistible bayonet attacks of their "ghazi" (heroes) and of thousands of Englishmen taken prisoner or chased back into the sea, whereas it was a well-known fact even in Pera that the retreat had been carried out in a most masterly way with practically no loss of life, and that the Turks themselves had been caught napping this time; but to lie is human, and the Turks owed it to their prestige to have an unmistakable and great military victory to form the basis of that "Holy War" that was so long in getting under weigh; and when all is said and done, their truly heroic defence really was a victory.

The absurd thing about all these lies was the way they were foisted on a public who already knew the true state of affairs and had nothing whatever to do with the "Holy War."

The Turks made even more of the second piece of good fortune that fell to their lot— the fall of Kut-el-Amara. General Townshend became their cherished prisoner, and was provided with a villa on the island of Halki in the Sea of Marmora, with a staff of Turkish naval officers to act as interpreters.

In the neighbouring and more fashionable Prinkipo he was received by practically everyone with open arms, and once even a concert was arranged in his honour, which was attended by the élite of Turkish and Levantine Society—the Turks because of their vanity and pride in their important prisoner of war, the Levantines because of their political sympathy with General Townshend, who, although there against his will, seemed to bring them a breath of that world they had lost all contact with for nearly two years and for which they longed with the most ardent and passionate desire.

On the occasion of the Bairam Festival—the highest Musulman festival—in 1916, the Turkish Government made a point of sending a group of about seventy Anglo-Indian Mohammedan officers, who had been taken prisoner at the fall of Kut and were now interned in Eski-Shehir, to the "Caliph City of Stamboul," where they were entertained for ten days in different Turkish hotels and shown everything that would seem to be of value for "Holy War" propaganda purposes.

I had the opportunity of conversing with some of these Indian officers in the garden of the "Petit Champs," where their appearance one evening made a most tremendous sensation. I had of course to be very discreet, for we were surrounded by spies, but I came away firmly convinced that, in spite of their good treatment, which was of course not without its purpose, and most unceasing and determined efforts to influence them, the Turkish propaganda so far as these Indian officers was concerned had entirely failed and that their loyalty to England remained absolutely unshaken. Will anyone blame me, if, angry and disgusted as I was at all these Turkish intrigues— it was shortly after that dramatic scene of the tortured Armenian which called forth that denunciation of Germany from my wife—I said to a group of these Indians—just this and nothing more!—that they should not believe all that the Turks told them, and that the result of the war would be very different from what the Turks thought? One of the officers thanked me with glowing eyes on behalf of his comrades and himself, and told me what a comfort my assurance was to them. They had nothing to complain of, he said, save being cut off from all news except official Turkish reports.

The very most that even the wildest fancy could find in events like Gallipoli and Kut-el-Amara was brought forward for the benefit of the "Holy War," but, despite everything, the propaganda was, as we have seen, a hopeless failure. Reverses such as the fall of Erzerum, Trebizond, and Ersindjan, on the contrary, which took place between the two above-mentioned victories, have never to this day been even so much as hinted at in the official war communiqués for the Ottoman public. For the communiqués for home and foreign consumption were always radically different.

It was not until very much later, when the Turkish counter-offensive against Bitlis seemed to be bearing fruit, that a few mild indications of these defeats were made in Parliament, with a careful suppression of all names, and the newspapers were empowered to make some mention of a "purely temporary retreat of no strategic importance" which had then taken place. The usual stereotyped report of 3,000 or 5,000 dead that was officially given out after every battle throughout the whole course of operations in the Irak scarcely came off in this case, however, and, to tell the truth,

Erzerum and these countless English dead reported in the Irak did more than anything else to undermine completely the people's already sadly shaken confidence in the official war communiqués.

If there was a real victory to be celebrated, the most stringent police orders were issued that flags were to be flown everywhere—on every building. Surely it is only in a land like Turkey that one could see the curious sight I witnessed after the fall of Bucharest—the victorious flags of the Central Powers, surmounted by the Turkish crescent, flying even from the balconies of Rumanian subjects, because there had been a definite police warning issued that, in the case of non-compliance with the order, the houses would be immediately ransacked and the families inhabiting them sent off to the interior of Anatolia. Under the circumstances, refusal to carry out police orders was impossible. That was the Turkish idea of the respect due to individual liberty.

This gives me an opportunity to say something of the treatment of prisoners. I may say in one word that it is, on the whole, good. Justice compels me to admit that the Turk, when he does take prisoners, treats them kindly and chivalrously; but he takes few prisoners, for he knows only too well how to wield his bayonet in those murderous charges he makes. Indeed, apart from the few hundred that fell into their hands in the Dardanelles or on the Russo-Turkish front, together with the crews of a few captured submarines, all the Turkish prisoners of war come from Kut-el-Amara. But the primitive Turk is all too sadly lacking in the comforts of life himself to be able to provide them for his prisoners. Without the help of the Commission that works under the protection of the American Embassy for the relief of the Entente prisoners, and sends piles of warm clothing, excellent shoes (which rouse the special envy of the Turks), chocolate, cakes, etc., to the Anatolian camps, these men, accustomed to European ways of life, would be in a sad plight.

The repeated and "humiliating marching of prisoners of war

through the streets of Constantinople to show them off to the childish gaze of a people much influenced by externals, might with advantage be dispensed with. And it was certainly not exactly kind to make wounded English officers process past the Sultan at the Friday's "Selamlik"; it was rather too like slave-driving methods and the abuses of the Middle Ages.

I was an unwilling witness of one most regrettable incident that took place shortly before I left Constantinople. In this case the sufferings of some unfortunate prisoners of war were cruelly exploited for political ends. A whole troup of about 2,000 Rumanians, from Dobrudja, were hounded up and down the streets of Pera and Stamboul in a purposely destitute and exhausted condition, so that the appearance of these poor wretches, who hung their heads dejectedly and had lost all trace of military bearing, might give the impression that the Turks were dealing with a very inferior foe and would soon be at the end of the business. This is how the authorities were going to increase the confidence of the doubting population!

The Turkish escort had apparently given these prisoners nothing to drink on the way— although the Turk, being a great water-drinker himself, knows only too well what a man needs on a dusty journey of several days on a transport train—for with my own eyes I saw dozens of them simply flinging themselves like animals full length on the ground when they reached the Taksim Fountain, and trying to slake their terrible thirst. It was with pitiable trickery like this— for which no doubt Enver Pasha was responsible, for the simple Turkish soldier is much too good-natured not to share his bread and water with his prisoners—that attempts were made, at the expense of all feelings of humanity, to cheer up the uneducated masses.

The Turkish Government, however, apart from a few cases of reprisals, where the prisoners were treated in an even more barbaric and primitive manner, did not, as a general rule, go the length of interning civilians. This was not without its own good grounds. In the first place, a very large part of the trade of the country lay in the hands of these Europeans, and they were consequently absolutely indispensable to the Turks in their everyday commercial life; secondly, a Government that had systematically rooted out the Armenians, hanged Arabian notables, and brutally mishandled the Greeks, could scarcely dispense, in the eyes of Europe, with the very last pretence of being more or less civilised; and, lastly, perhaps the fear of being brought to book later on may have had a restraining influence on them—we saw how growing anxiety about the Russian advance on the Eastern front led, at any rate for a time, to a discontinuance of Armenian persecutions.

Besides all this, hundreds and thousands of Turks were resident in enemy countries, and of course the desire was to avoid reprisals. So the Government contented itself with threats and subterfuges, after a first unsuccessful attempt to expose a large number of French subjects to fire from the enemy guns in Gallipoli—a plan which failed entirely, owing to the energetic opposition of officials of the American Embassy who had accompanied these chosen victims to Gallipoli. Every means was used, however, even announcements in the newspapers and a Vote of Credit "for the removal of enemy subjects to the interior," to keep the sword of Damocles for ever hanging over the heads of all subjects of Entente countries, even women and children.

From the fall of Kut-el-Amara up to the time of Rumania's entry into the war, there were no important episodes of a military or political nature from the particular point of view of Turkey. (The Arabian catastrophe I will deal with in another connection.) With the ebb and flow of war and constant anxiety about Russia's movements, time passed slowly enough. It was well known that the Turkish offensive was already considerably weakened and the lack of means of transport was an open secret. Starvation and spotted fever raged at the Front as well as in the interior and the capital.

Asiatic cholera even made its appearance in European Pera, but was fortunately successfully combated by vaccination.

Further decisive Russian victories on the west and the Gulf of Alexandretta were expected after the fall of Ersindjian, for the ambition and personal hatred against the Turks of the Grand Duke Nicolai Nicolajivitch, commanding the armies in Armenia, would probably stop short at nothing less than complete overthrow of the enemy. Simple-minded souls, whose geography was not their strong point, reckoned how long it would take the Russians to get from Anatolia and when the conquest of Constantinople would take place.

The less optimistic among those who were panting for final emancipation from the Young Turkish military yoke set their hopes on the entry of Rumania. In all circles Rumania's probable attitude was fairly clear, and no one ever doubted that she would be drawn into the war.

In consequence of the new operations after Rumania's declaration of war, the revival of the offensive in Macedonia, and the events in Athens, all eyes were turned again to the ever-doubtful Greece. The Greek element, Ottoman and Hellenic combined, in Constantinople alone may be reckoned at several hundred thousand. Never were sympathies so great for Venizelos, never was the spirit of the Irredenta so outspoken as among the Greeks in Turkey, who had been the dupes since 1909 of every possible kind of Young Turkish intrigue. In contrast to the Armenians, the great mass of whom thought and felt as loyal Ottoman citizens right up to the very end when Talaat and Enver's policy of extermination set in against them—in contrast to these absolutely helpless and therefore all the more easy victims to the Turkish national lust of persecution, the attitude of the Greek citizens was all the more marked.

Since the Greeco-Turkish war of 1912-13 and the impetus given to Pan-Hellenism by the successful issue of the war, there is not one single Greek in either country—no matter what his social standing—that has not ardently looked forward to and desired the overthrow of Turkey. But the Greek is much too clever to let his feelings be seen; and he is not so unprotected as the Armenian. And so up to the present time the Turk has confined himself more to small intrigues against the Greek population, except in a few remote districts— more especially the shores of the Black Sea— where massacres like those organised among the Armenians have been carried out, but on a very much smaller scale.

Sympathy with Venizelos and the Irredentistic desire for Greece to throw in her lot with the Entente are counterbalanced, however, in the case of the Greeks living in Turkey, by grave anxiety as to their own welfare if it came to a break between the two countries. Turkish hatred of the Greeks knows no bounds, and it was no idle fear that made the Greeks in Constantinople tremble, in spite of their satisfaction politically, when the rumours were afloat in autumn 1916 of King Constantine's abdication and Greece's entry on the side of the Entente.

But the ideas as to how the Turks would act towards them in such a case were diametrically opposed even among those who had lived in the country a long time and knew the Turkish mind exactly. Many expected immediate Greek massacres on the largest scale; others, again, expected only brutal intrigues and chicanery, economic ruin; still others thought that nothing at all would happen, that the Turks were already too demoralised, and that at any rate in Pera the far superior Greek element would completely command the situation. This last I considered mere megalomaniac optimism in view of the fact that Turkey was still unbroken so far as things military were concerned, and I believe that those people were right who believed that Greece's entry on the side of the Entente would be the signal for the carrying out of atrocities against all Greeks, at any rate in the commercial world.

It would be interesting to know which idea the German authorities favoured. That the event would pass off without damage being done, they apparently did not believe, for in those days when Greece's decision seemed to be imminent, the former Goeben and the Breslau, which had been lying at Stenia on the Bosporus, were brought up with all speed and anchored just off the coast with their guns turned on Pera, and the German garrison, as I knew from different officers, had orders to be prepared for an alarm.

Did the Germans think they were going to have to protect Turks or Greeks in the case of definite news from Athens? Was it Germany's intention to protect the European population, who had nothing to do with the impending political decision, although they might sympathise with it—was it Germany's intention to protect them, at any rate in this instance, from the Turkish lust of extermination? Had these two ships, now known as the Jawuz Sultan Selim and the Midilli, not belonged for a long time to the Imperial Ottoman Navy?

When Rumania flung off her shackles, there was great rejoicing in Pera, and even the greatest pessimists believed that relief was near and would be accomplished within two months at latest. But another and more terrible reverse absolutely destroyed the last shred of anti-Turkish hope, and the victories in Rumania, especially the fall of Bucharest, combined with the speech of the Russian minister Trepoff, had the effect of sending over solid to the side of the Government even the few who had hitherto, at least in theory, formed an opposition, although a powerless one.

Victories shared with the Bulgarians, too, did away with the last remains of unfriendly feelings towards that people and consolidated the Turko-Bulgarian Alliance. Indeed, one may say that for Turkey the third great phase of the war began with the removal of all danger of the fall of Constantinople through the collapse of the Rumanian forces.

The first comprised the time of the powerful attacks directed at the very heart of the Empire, its most vulnerable point, and ended with the English-French evacuation of Gallipoli. The second was the period of alternate successes and reverses, almost a time of stagnation, when practically all interest was centred on the Russian menace in Asia Minor and the efforts made to withstand it. It ended equally successfully with the removal of the Russian menace from the Balkans. The third will be the phase of increasing internal weakness, of the dissipation of strength through the sending of troops to Europe, of the successful renewal of the English offensive in Mesopotamia, perhaps even of an English-French offensive against Syria and of the final revolt of all the Arabian lands, ushered in by the events in the Hedjaz and the founding of a purely Arabian Caliphate. The third phase cannot last longer than the year 1917; it will mean the decision of the whole European war.

CHAPTER V

During the entire course of the war as I have briefly sketched it in the foregoing pages, the economic situation in the whole country and particularly in the capital became more and more serious. But, let me just say here, in anticipation, that Turkey, being a purely agricultural country with a very modest population, can never be brought to sue for peace through starvation, nor, with Germany backing and financing her, through any general exhaustion of commercial resources, until Germany herself is brought to her knees. Any victory must be a purely military and political one. The whole crux of the food problem in Turkey is that the people suffer, suffer cruelly, but not enough for hunger to have any results in the shape of an earlier conclusion of peace. This is the case also with the Central Powers, as the Entente have unfortunately only too surely convinced themselves now after their first illusions to the contrary.

There is another element in the Turkish question too—the large majority of the population are a heterogeneous mass of enslaved and degenerate beings, outcasts of society, plunged in the lowest social and commercial depths, entirely lacking in all initiative, who can never become a factor in any political upheaval, for in Turkey this can only be looked for from the military or the educated classes. If the Entente Powers ever counted on Turkey's chronic state of starvation and lack of supplies coming to their aid in this war, they have made a sad mistake. Therefore in attempting to sketch in a few pages the conditions of life and the economic situation in Turkey, my aim is solely to bring to light the underlying Turkish methods, and the ethics and spirit of the Young Turkish Government.

During the periods of the very acute bread crises, which occurred more than once, but notably in the beginning of 1916, some dozen men literally died of hunger daily in Constantinople alone. With my own eyes I have repeatedly seen women collapsing from exhaustion in the streets. From many parts of the interior, particularly Syria, there were reliable reports of a still worse state of affairs. But even in more normal times there was always a difficulty in obtaining bread, for the means of communication in that vast and primitive land of Turkey are precarious at best, and it was no easy matter to get the grain transported to the centres of consumption.

Then in Constantinople there was a shortage not only of skilled labour, but of coal for milling purposes. The result was that the townspeople only received a daily ration of a quarter of a kilogramme (about 8 oz. — not a quarter of an oka, which would be about 10 oz.) of bread, which was mostly of an indigestible and occasionally very doubtful quality — utterly uneatable by Europeans — although occasionally it was quite good though coarse. If the poor people in Constantinople wanted to supplement this very insufficient allowance, they could do so when things were in a flourishing condition at the price of about 2 1/2 or 3 piastres (1 piastre = about 2 1/4 d.) the English pound, and later 4 or 5 piastres. Even this was for the most part only procurable by clandestine means from soldiers who were usually willing to turn part of their bread ration into money.

This is about all that can be said about the feeding of the people, for bread is by far the most important food of the Oriental, and the prices of the other foodstuffs soon reached exorbitant heights. What were the poor to feed on when rice, reckoned in English coinage, cost roughly from 3s. 2d. to 4s. 4d. an oka (about 2 1/2 lb.), beans 2s. 4d. the oka, meat 3s. to 4s., and the cheapest sheep's cheese and olives, hitherto the most common Turkish condiment to eat with bread, rose to 3s. and 1s. 8d. the oka?

Wages, on the other hand, were ludicrously low. We may obtain some idea of the standard of living from the fact that the Government, who always favoured the soldiers, did not pay more than 5 piastres (about 1s.) a day to the families of soldiers on active service. I have often wondered what the people really did eat, and I was never able to come to any satisfactory conclusion, although I often went to market myself to buy and see what other people bought. It is significant enough that just shortly before I left Constantinople—that is, a few weeks after the Turko-Bulgarian-German victories in Rumania and the fall of Bucharest—the price of bread in the Turkish capital, in spite of the widely advertised "enormous supplies" taken in Rumania, rose still higher.

I cannot speak from personal experience of what happened after Christmas 1916 in this connection, but everyone was quite convinced, in spite of the official report, that the harvest of 1916, despite the tremendous and praiseworthy efforts of the Ministry of Agriculture and the military authorities, would show a very marked decrease as a result of the mobilisation of agricultural labour, the requisitioning of implements, and the shortage of buffaloes, which, instead of ploughing fields, were pulling guns over the snow-covered uplands of Armenia. There was a very general idea that the harvest of 1917 would be a horrible catastrophe. And yet I am fully convinced, and I must emphasise it again, that, in spite of agricultural disaster, Turkey will still go on as a military power.

And now let us see what the Government did in connection with the food problem. At a comparatively early stage they followed Germany's example and introduced bread tickets, which were quite successful so long as the flour lasted. In the autumn of 1915 they took the organisation of the bread supply for large towns out of the hands of the municipalities, and gave it over to the War Office. They got Parliament to vote a large fund to buy up all available supplies of flour, and in view of the immense importance of bread as the chief means of nourishment of the masses, they decided to sell it at a very considerable loss to themselves, so that the price of the daily ration (though not of the supplementary ration) remained very much as it had been in peace time. The Government always favoured the purely Mohammedan quarters of the town so far as bread supply was concerned, and the people living in Fatih and other parts of Stamboul were very much better off than the inhabitants of Græco-European Pera.

Then Talaat made speeches in the House on the food question in which he did all in his power to throw dust in the eyes of the starving population, but he did not really succeed in blinding anyone as to the true state of affairs. In February 1916, when there was practically a famine in the land, he even went so far as to declare in Parliament that the food supplies for the whole of Turkey had been so increased by enormous purchases in Rumania, that they were now fully assured for two years.

It was no doubt with cynical enjoyment that the "Committee" of the Young Turks enlarged on the privations of the people in such publications as the semi-official Tanin, in which the following wonderful sentiment appeared: One can pass the night in relative brightness without oil in one's lamp if one thinks of the bright and glorious future that this war is preparing for Turkey!"

One could have forgiven such cheap phrases if they had been a true, though possibly misguided, attempt to provide comfort in face of real want; but at the same time as such paragraphs were appearing in the Tallin and thousands of poor Turkish households had to spend the long winter nights without the slightest light, thousands of tons of oil were lying in Constantinople alone in the stores of the official accapareurs.

This brings me to the second series of measures taken by the Turkish Government to relieve the economic situation—those of a negative nature. Their positive measures are pretty well exhausted when one has mentioned their treatment of the bread crisis.

The question of requisitioning is one of the most important in Turkish life in wartime, and is not without its ludicrous side. In imitation of German war-time methods, either wrongly understood or wittingly misapplied by Oriental greed, the Turkish Government requisitioned pretty well everything in the food line or in the shape of articles of daily use that were sure to be scarce and would necessarily rise in price. But while in the civilised countries of Central Europe the supplies so requisitioned were sagely applied to the general good, the members of the "Committee of Union and Progress" looked with fine contempt and the grim cynicism of arch-dictators on the privations and sufferings of the people so long as they did not actually starve, and used the supplies requisitioned for the personal enrichment of their clique.

When I speak of requisitioning, I do not mean the necessary military carrying off of grain, cattle, vehicles, buffaloes, and horses, general equipment, and so on, in exchange for a scrap of paper to be redeemed after the war (of very doubtful value in view of Turkey's position) —I do not mean that, even though the way it was accomplished bled the country far more than was necessary, falling as it did in the country districts into the hands of ignorant, brutal, and fanatical underlings, and in the town being carried out with every kind of refinement by the central authorities. Too often it was a means of violent "nationalisation" and deprivation of property and rights exercised especially against Armenians, Greeks, and subjects of other Entente countries. If there was a particularly nice villa or handsome estate belonging to someone who was not a Turk, soldiers were immediately billeted there under some pretext or other, and it was not long before these rough Anatolians had reduced everything to rack and ruin.

I do not mean either the terrible damage to commercial life brought about by the way the military authorities, in complete disregard of agricultural interests, were always seizing railway waggons, and so completely laming all initiative on the part of farmers and merchants, whose goods were usually simply emptied out on the spot, exposed to ruin, or disposed of without any kind of compensation being given. What I do mean is the huge semi-official cornering of food, which must be regarded as typical of the Young Turks' idea of their official responsibility towards those for whom they exercised stewardship.

The "Bakal Clique" ("provision merchants," "grocers") was known through the whole of Constantinople, and was keenly criticised by the much injured public. It was, first of all, under the official patronage of the city prefect, Ismet Bey, a creature of the Committee; but later on, when they realised that dire necessity made a continuance of this system of cornering quite unthinkable, he was made the scapegoat, and his dismissal from office was freely commented on in the Committee newspapers as "an act of deliverance." The Committee thought that they would thus throw dust in the eyes of the sorely-tried people of Constantinople. Hundreds of thousands of Turkish pounds were turned into cash in the shortest possible time by this semi-official syndicate, at the expense of the starving population, and found their way into the pockets of the administrators.

That was how the Young Turkish parvenus were able to fulfil their one desire and wriggle their way into the best clubs, where they gambled away huge sums of money. The method was simple enough: whatever was eatable or useable, but could only be obtained by import from abroad, was "taken charge of," and starvation rations, which were simply ludicrously inadequate and quite insufficient for the needs of even the poorest household, were doled out by "vesikas" (the ticket system).

The great stock of goods, however, was sold secretly at exorbitant prices by the creatures of the "Bakal Clique," who simply cornered the market. That is how it happened that in Constantinople, cut off as it was from the outer world and without imports, even at the end of 1916, with a population of well over a million, there were still unlimited stores of everything available for those who could pay fancy prices, while by the beginning of 1915 those less well endowed with worldly goods had quite forgotten the meaning of comfort and the poor were starving with ample stores of everything still available.

In businesses belonging to enemy subjects the system of requisitioning, of course, reached a climax, stores of all kinds worth thousands of pounds simply disappearing, without any reason being given for carrying them off, and nothing offered in exchange, but one of these famous "scraps of paper." Cases have been verified and were freely discussed in Pera of ladies' shoes and ladies' clothing even being requisitioned and turned into large sums of cash by the consequent rise in price.

The profiteering of Ismet and company, who chose the specially productive centre of the capital for their system of usury, was not, however, by any means an isolated case of administrative corruption, for exactly the same system of requisitioning, holding up and then reselling under private management at as great a profit as possible, underlay and underlies the great semi-official Young Turkish commercial organisation, with branches throughout the whole country, known as the "Djemiet" and under the distinguished patronage of Talaat himself.

After Ismet Bey's fall, the "Djemiet" took over the supplying of the capital as well (with the exception of bread). We will speak elsewhere of this great organisation, which is established not only for war purposes, but serves towards the nationalisation of economic life. So far as the system of requisitioning is concerned, it comes into the picture through its firm opposition to German merchants who were trying to buy up stores of food and raw materials from their ally Turkey. The intrigues and counter-intrigues on both sides sometimes had most remarkable results.

One of the really bright sides of life in Constantinople in wartime was the amusement one extracted from the silent and desperate war continually being waged by the many well-fed gentlemen of the "Z.E.G." {"Zentralein-kaufsgesellschaft" "Central Purchasing Commission") and their minions who tried to rob Turkey of foodstuffs and raw material for the benefit of Germany, against the "Djemiet" and more particularly the Quartermaster-General, Ismail Hakki Pasha, that wooden-legged, enormously wealthy representative of the neo-Turkish spirit—he was the most perfect blend of Oriental politeness and narrow-minded decision to do exactly the opposite of what he had promised. On the Turkish side, the determination to safeguard the interests of the Army, and in the case of the "Djemiet" the effort not to let any foodstuffs out of Germany—a standpoint that has at last found expression in a formal prohibition of all export—then the quest of personal enrichment on the part of the great "Clique"; on the German side, the insatiable hunger for everything Turkey could provide that had been lacking for a long time in Germany: the whole thing was a wonderfully variegated picture of mutual intrigue.

The gentlemen of the "Z.E.G.," after months of inactivity spent in reviling the Turks and studying Young Turkish and other morals and manners by frequenting all the pleasure resorts in the place, managed at last to get the exports of raw materials set on the right road, and so it came about that the fabulous sums in German money that had to be put into circulation in payment of these goods, in spite of Turkey's indebtedness to Germany, led to a very considerable depreciation in the value of the Mark even in Turkey for some time.

But until the understanding as to exports was finally arrived at, there were many dramatic events in Constantinople, culminating in the Turks re-requisitioning, with the help of armed detachments, stores already paid for by Germany and lying in the warehouses of the "Z.E.G. and the German Bank!

On the financial side, apart from Turkey's enormous debt to Germany, the wonderful attempt at a reform and standardisation of the coinage in the middle of May 1916 is worthy of mention. The reform, which was a simplification of huge economic value of the tremendously complicated money system and introducing a theoretical gold unit, must be regarded chiefly as a war measure to prevent the rapid deterioration of Turkish paper money.

This last attempt, as was obvious after a few months' trial, was entirely unsuccessful, and even hastened the fall of paper money, for the population soon discovered at the back of these drastic measures the thinly veiled anxiety of the Government lest there should be a further deterioration. Dire punishments, such as the closing down of money-changers' businesses and arraignment before a military court for the slightest offence, were meted out to anyone found guilty of changing gold or even silver for paper.

In November 1916, however, it was an open secret that, in spite of all these prohibitions, there was no difficulty in the inland provinces and in Syria and Palestine in changing a gold pound for two or more paper pounds. In still more unfrequented spots no paper money would be accepted, so that the whole trade of the country simply came to a standstill. Even in Constantinople at the beginning of December 1916, paper stood to gold as 100 to 175.

The Anatolian population still went gaily on. burying all the available silver medjidichs and even nickel piastres in their clay pots in the ground, because being simple country folk they could not understand, as the Government with all its prayers and threats were so anxious they should, that throughout Turkey and in the greater and mightier and equally victorious Germany, guaranteed paper money was really much better than actual coins, and was just as valuable as gold! The people, too, could not but remember what had happened with the "Kaimé" after the Turko-Russian war, when thousands who had believed in the assurances of the Government suddenly found themselves penniless. In Constantinople it was a favourite joke to take one of the new pound, half-pound, or quarter-pound notes issued under German paper, not gold, guarantee and printed only on one side and say, "This [pointing to the right side] is the present value, and that [blank side] will be the value on the conclusion of peace."

Even those who were better informed, however, and sat at the receipt of custom, did exactly the same as these stupid Anatolian country-people; no idea of patriotism prevented them from collecting everything metal they could lay their hands on, and, in spite of all threats of punishment—which could never overtake them!—paying the highest price in paper money for every gold piece they could get. Their argument was: "One must of course have something to live on in the time directly following the conclusion of peace." In ordinary trade and commerce, filthy, torn paper notes, down to a paper piastre, came more and more to be practically the only exchange.

A discerning Turk said to me once: "It would be a very good plan sometime to have the police search these great men for bullion every evening on their return from the official exchanges. That would be more to the point than any reform in the coinage!"

Those who could not get gold, bought roubles, which were regarded as one of the very best speculations going, until one day the Turkish Government, in their annoyance at some Russian victory, suddenly deported to Anatolia a rich Greek banker of the name of Vlasdari, who was accused of having speculated in roubles, which of course gave them the double benefit of getting rid of a Greek and seizing his beautiful estate in Pera.

Only the greatest optimists were deceived into believing that it was a profitable transaction to buy Austrian paper money at the fabulously low price the Austrian Krone had reached against the Turkish pound, which was really neither politically nor financially in any better a state. The members of the "Committee of Union and Progress" had of course shipped their gold off to Switzerland long ago.

CHAPTER VI

German propaganda and ethics — The unsuccessful "Holy War" and the German Government — "The Holy War" a crime against civilisation, a chimera, a farce — Underhand dealings — The German Embassy the dupe of adventurers — The morality of German Press representatives — A trusty servant of the German Embassy — Fine official distinctions of morality — The German conception of the rights of individuals.

Now that we have given a rough sketch of the main events of the war as it affected the economic life of the people, and have devoted a chapter to that sinister crime, the Armenian persecutions, we shall leave the Young Turks for a moment and turn to an examination of German propaganda methods.

It is a very painful task for a German who does not profess to be a "World Politician," but really thinks in terms of true "world-politics," to deal with the many intrigues and machinations of our Government in their relation to the so-called "Holy War" (Arab. Djihad), where in their quest of a vain illusion they stooped to the very lowest means. Practically all their hopes in that direction have been sadly shattered. Their costly, unscrupulous, thoroughly unmoral efforts against European civilisation in Mohammedan countries have resulted in the terrific counter-stroke of the defection of the Arabs and the foundation of a purely Arabian Chaliphate under English protection. Thus England has already won a brilliant victory against Germany and Turkey in spite of Gallipoli and Kut-el-Amara, although it seems probable that even these will be wiped out by greater deeds on the part of the Entente before long. One could not have a better example of Germany's total inability to succeed in the sphere of world-politics.

The so-called "Holy War," if it had succeeded, would have been one of the greatest crimes against human civilisation that even Germany has on her conscience, remembering as we do her recent ruthless "frightfulness" at sea, and her attempt to set Mexico and the Japanese against the land of most modern civilisation and of greatest liberty. A successful "Djihad" spreading to all the lands of Islam would have set back by years all that civilisation so patiently and so painfully won; it would not have been at all comparable with the Entente's use of coloured troops in Europe which Germany deprecated so loudly, for in the Holy War it would have been a case of letting the wildest fanaticism loose against the armies of law and order and civilisation; in the case of the Entente it was part of a purely military action on the part of England and France, who held under their sway all the inhabitants, coloured and otherwise, of those Colonial regions from which troops were sent to Europe and to which they will return.

But the attempt against colonial civilisation did not succeed. The "Djihad," proclaimed as it was by the Turanian pseudo-Chaliph and violently anti-Entente, was doomed to failure from the very start from its obvious artificiality. It was a miserable farce, or rather a tragicomedy, the present ending of which, namely the defection of the Arabian Chaliphate, is the direct contrary of what had been aimed at with such fanatical urgency and the use of such immoral propaganda.

The attempt to "unloose" the Holy War was due primarily to the most absurd illusions. It would seem that in Germany, the land of science, the home of so many eminent doctors of research, even the scholars have been attacked by that disease of being dazzled by wild political illusions, or surely, knowing the countries of Islam outside-in as they must, they would long ago have raised their voices against such arrant folly. It would seem that all her inherent knowledge, all her studies, have been of little or no avail to Germany, so that mistake after mistake has been committed in the realm of world politics. It may be said that Germany, even if she were doubtful of the issue, should still not have left untried this means of crippling her opponents. To that I can only reply by pointing to the actual position of affairs, well known to Germany, not only in English, but also in French and Russian Islamic colonial territory, which should have rendered the "Djihad" entirely and absolutely out of the question.

Let us take for example Egypt, French North-West Africa, and Russian Turkestan, not to speak of the masterly English colonial rule in India, which has now been tested and tried for centuries. Anyone who has ever seen Egypt with the area under culture practically doubled under modern English rule by the help of every kind of technical contrivance for the betterment of existing conditions, and the skilful utilisation of all available means at an expense of millions of pounds, with its needy population given an opportunity to earn a living wage and even wealth through a lucrative cultivation of the land under conditions that are a paradise compared with what they were under the Turkish rule of extortion and despotism—anyone who has seen that must have looked from the very beginning with a very doubtful eye on Germany's and Turkey's illusions of stirring up these well-doing people against their rulers.

The same thing occurs again in the extended territory of North-West Africa from the Atlas lands to the Guinea coast and Lake Chad, where France, as I know from personal experience, stands on a high level of colonial excellence, developing all the resources of the country with consummate skill, shaping her "empire colonial" more and more into a shining gem in the crown of colonial endeavour, and, as I can testify from my own observations in Morocco, Senegal, the Niger, and the Interior of the Guinea territories of the "A.O.F." (Afrique Occidentale Francaise), capturing the hearts of the whole population by her essential culture, and, last but not least, winning the Mohammedans by her clever Islam policy.

That, finally, Russia, at any rate from the psychological standpoint, is perhaps the best coloniser of Further Asia, even German textbooks on colonial policy admit unreservedly, and the glowing conditions that she has brought about especially in the basin of Ferghana in Turkestan by the introduction of the flourishing and lucrative business of cotton-growing are known to everyone. Only politicians of the most wildly fantastic type, who see everywhere what they want to see, could believe that in this war the Turkish "Turanistic" bait would ever have any effect in Russian Central Asia, or make its inhabitants now living in security, peace, and well-being wish back again the conditions which prevailed under the Emirs of Samarkand, Khiva, and Bokhara. But Germany, who should have been well informed if anyone was, believed all these fantastic impossibilities.

One could let it pass with a slight feeling of irritation against Germany if it were merely a case of the failure of the "Djihad." But unfortunately the propaganda, as stupid as it was unsuccessful, exercised in this connection, will be written down for all time as one of the blackest and most despicable marks against Germany's account in this war. In Turkey alone, the underhand manipulation for the unloosing of the "Holy War" and the German Press propaganda so closely allied with it, indeed the whole way in which the German cause in the East was represented journalistically throughout the war, are subjects full of the saddest, most biting irony, to sympathise with which must lower every German who has lived in the Turkish capital in the eyes of the whole civilised world.

In order to demonstrate the role played in this affair by the German Embassy at Constantinople I will not make an exhaustive survey but simply confine myself to a few episodes and outstanding features. An eminent German Red Cross doctor, clear-sighted and reliable, who had many tales to tell of what he had seen in the "Caucasus" campaign, said to me one evening, as we sat together at a promenade concert: "Do you see that man in Prussian major's uniform going past? I met him twice in Erzerum last winter. The man was nothing but an employee in a merchant's business in

Baku, and had learnt Russian there. He has never done military service. When war broke out, he hurried to the Embassy in Pera and offered his services to stir up the Georgians and other peoples of the Caucasus against Russia. Of course he got full powers to do what he wanted, and guns and ammunition and piles of propaganda pamphlets were placed at his disposal so that he might carry on his work from the frontier of the then still neutral Turkey. Whole chests full of good gold coins were sent to him to be distributed confidentially for propaganda purposes; of course he was his own most confidential friend! He went back to Erzerum without having won a single soul for the cause of the 'Djihad.' That has not prevented his living as a 'grand seigneur,' for the Embassy are not yet daunted, and now the fellow struts about in a major's uniform, lent to him, although he has never been a soldier, so that the cause may gain still more prestige."

Numerous examples of similar measures might be cited, and instances without number given, of the German Embassy being made the dupe of greedy adventurers who treated them as an inexhaustible source of gold. First one would appear on the scene who announced himself as the one man to cope with Afghanistan, then another would come along on his way to Persia and play the great man "on a special mission" for a time in Pera while money belonging to the German Empire would find its way into all sorts of low haunts. And so things went on for two years until, with the Arabian catastrophe, even the eyes of the great diplomatic optimists of Ayas-Pasha might have been opened.

I will only mention here how even a bona fide connoisseur of the East like Baron von Oppenheim, who had already made tours of considerable value for research purposes right across the Arabian Peninsula, and so should have known better than to share these false illusions, doled out thousands of marks from his own pocket—and millions from the Treasury!—to stir up the "tribes to take part in the "Djihad," and how he returned to Pera from his propaganda tour with a real Bedouin beard, and, still unabashed, took over the control of the German Embassy's "News Bureau," which kept up these much-derided war telegraph and picture offices known in Pera and elsewhere by the non-German populace as sacs de mensonges, and which flooded the whole of the East with waggon loads of pamphlets in every conceivable tongue—in fact these, with guns and ammunition, formed the chief load of the bi-weekly "culture-bringing" Balkan train!

I will only cite the one example of the far-famed Mario Passarge—a real Apache to look at. With his friend Frobenius, the ethnographer and German agent, well known to me personally from French West Africa for his liking for absinthe and negro women and his Teutonic brusqueness emphasised in comparison with the kindly, helpful French officials, as well as by hearsay from many scandalous tales, Passarge undertook that disastrous expedition to the Abyssinians which failed so lamentably owing to the Italians, and then after its collapse came to Turkey as special correspondent of the Vossische Zeitung and managed to swindle his way through Macedonia with a false Italian passport to Greece, where he wrote sensational reports for his wonderful newspaper about the atrocities and low morale of Sarrail's army—the same newspaper that had made itself the laughing-stock of the whole of Europe, and at the same time had managed to get the German Government to pursue for two years the shadow of a separate peace with Russia, by publishing a marvellous series of "Special Reports via Stockholm," on conditions in Russia that were nothing but a tissue of lies inspired by blind Jewish hate; if a tithe of them had been true, Russia would have gone under long ago.

I need not repeat my own opinion on all the machinations of the German Embassy, but I will simply give you word for word what a German Press agent in Constantinople (I will mention no names) once said to me: "It is unbelievable," he declared, "what a mob of low characters frequent the German Embassy now. The scum of the earth, people who would never have dared before the war to have been seen on the pavements of Ayas-Pasha, have now free entry.

Any day you can see some doubtful-looking character accosting the porter at the Embassy, whispering something in his ear, and then being ushered down the steps to where the propaganda department, the news bureau, has its quarters. There he gives wonderful assurances of what he can do, and promises to stir up some Mohammedan people for the "Djihad." Then he waits a while in the ante-room, and is finally received by the authorities ; but the next time he comes to the Embassy he walks in through the well-carpeted main entrance, and requests an audience with the Ambassador or other high official, and we soon find him comfortably equipped and setting off on a 'special mission' as the confidential servant of the German Embassy." But even the recognition of these truths has not prevented this journalist from eating from the crib of the German Embassy!

I cannot leave this disagreeable subject without making some mention of a type that does more than anything to throw light on the morale of this German propaganda. Everyone in Constantinople knows—or rather knew, for he has now feathered his nest comfortably and departed to Germany with his money— Mehmed Zekki "Bey," the publisher and chief editor of the military paper Die Nationalver-teidigung and its counterpart La Défense, published daily in French but representative of Young Turkish-German interests. Hundreds of those who know Zekki also know that he used to be called "Capitaine Nelken y Waldberg." Fewer know that "Nelken" alone would have been more in accordance with fact. I will relate the history of this individual, as I know it from the mouths of reliable informants—the members of the Embassy and the Consulate. Nelken, a Roumanian Jew, a shopkeeper by trade, had been several times in prison for bankruptcy and fraud, and at last fled from Roumania. He took refuge in the Turkish capital, where he continued his business and married a Greek wife. Here again he became bankrupt, as is only too clear from the public notice of restoration in the Constantinople newspapers, when his lucrative political activity as the champion of Krupp's, of the German cause and "the holy German war," as much a purely pan-

Germanic as Islamic affair, provided him with the wherewithal to pay off his former disreputable debts.

To go back to his history—with money won by fraud in his pocket, he deserted his wife and went off, no doubt having made a thorough and most professional study of the subject in the low haunts of Pera, as a white-slave trader to the Argentine, and then—I rely for my information on an official of the German Consulate in Pera—set up as proprietor of a brothel in Buenos Ayres. Then, as often happens, the Argentine special police took him into their service, thinking, on the principle of "setting a thief to catch a thief," that he would have special experience for the post. Grounds enough there for him to add on the second name of his falsified passport "Nelken y Waldberg" and to call himself in Europe a "Capitaine de la Gendarmerie" from the Argentine.

From there he went to Cairo and edited a little private paper called Les Petites Nouvelles Egyptiennes. For repeated extortion he was sentenced to one year's imprisonment, but unfortunately only in contumaciam, for he had already fled the country, not, however, before he had been publicly smacked on the face in the "Flasch" beer garden without offering satisfaction as an "Argentine General" should —a performance that was later repeated in every detail in Toklian's Restaurant in Constantinople.

He told me once that he had been sentenced in this way because, on an understanding with the then German Diplomatic Agent in Cairo, von Miquel, he had attacked Lord Cromer's policy sharply, and that his patron von Miquel had given him the timely hint to leave Egypt. I will leave it to one's imagination to discover how much truth there was in this former brothel-keeper's connection with official German "world-politics" and high diplomacy. From what I have seen personally since, I believe that Zekki, alias Nelken, was probably speaking the truth in this case, although it is certainly a fact that in German circles in Cairo at that time ordinary extortion was recognised as being punishable by imprisonment for a considerable length of time.

Nelken then returned to Constantinople and devoted himself with unflagging energy to his previous business of agent. He turned to the Islamic faith and became a citizen of the Ottoman Empire because he found it more profitable so to do, and could thus escape from his former liabilities. Then in spite of lack of means, he managed to found a military newspaper, which, however, soon petered out. Nelken became Mehmed Zekki and a journalist, and of course called himself "Bey.

Up to this point the history of this individual is nothing but a characteristic extract from life as it is lived by hundreds of rogues in the East. But now we come to something which is almost unbelievable and which leads me to give credence to his version of his relations with von Miquel, which after all only shows more clearly than ever that German "world-politics" are not above making use of the scum of the earth for their intrigues. In full knowledge of this man's whole black past—as Dr. Weber of the German Embassy himself told me—the German Embassy with the sanction of the Imperial Government (this I know from letters Zekki showed me in great glee from the Foreign Office and the War Office) appointed this fellow, whom all Pera said they would not touch with gloves on or with the tongs, to be their confidential agent with a large monthly honorarium and to become a pillar of "the German cause" in the East. And it could not even be said in extenuation that the man had any great desire or any wonderful vocation to represent Germany, for—as the Embassy official said to me—"We knew that Zekki was a dangerous character and rather inclined to the Entente at the outbreak of war, so we decided to win him over by giving him a salary rather than drive him into the enemy's camp." So it simply comes to this, that Germany buys a bankrupt, a blackmailer, a procurer, a brothel-keeper with cash to fight her "Holy War" for her!

As publisher of the Defense Zekki received a large salary from Germany, one from Austria, afterwards cut down not from any excess of moral sense, but simply from excess of economy, and a very considerable sum from Krupp's. As representative of German interests he did all he could to propitiate the Young Turks by the most fulsome flattery, and more recently he was pushing hard to get on the Committee of Union and Progress. But the Turks jibbed at what the German Embassy had brought on themselves—seeing Zekki "Bey" moving about their sacred halls with the most imposing nonchalance and condescension. Zekki himself once complained to me bitterly that in spite of his having presented Enver Pasha with a valuable clock worth eighty Turkish pounds which Enver had accepted with pleasure, he would not even answer a written request from Zekki craving an audience with him. (This, incidentally, is a most excellent example of the working of Enver's mind, a megalomaniac as greedy as he was proud.)

The military director of the Turkish Press said to me once: "We are only waiting for the first 'gaffe' in his paper to get this filthy creature hunted out of his lair," and one day when through carelessness a small uncensored and really quite harmless military notice appeared in print (everything is submitted to the censor), the Turkish Government gave it short shrift indeed, and banned sine die this "Ottoman" paper which lived by Krupp and the German trade advertisements, and had become an advocate of the German Embassy, because it was paid in good solid cash for it. The paper was replaced by a new one in Turkish hands, called Le Soir.

I could go on talking for ages from most intimate personal knowledge about this man, superb in his own way. His doings were not without a certain comic side which amused while it aggravated one. I could mention, for example, his great lawsuit in Germany in 1916, in which he brought an accusation of libel against some German who had called him a blackmailer and a criminal who had been repeatedly punished. He managed to win the lawsuit—that is, the defenders had to pay a fine of twenty marks, because the evidence brought against Zekki could not be followed up to Egypt on account of England's supremacy on the sea, and also no doubt because the interests of Krupp and the German Embassy could not have this cherished blossom of German propaganda disturbed! So for him at any rate the lack of "freedom of the seas" he had so often raged about in his leading articles was a very appreciable advantage.

The last time I remember seeing the man he was engaged in an earnest tête-à-tête about the propagation of German political interests by means of arms with the Nationalist Reichstag deputy, Dr. Streesemann, a representative of the German heavy goods trade and of German jingoism who had hastened to Constantinople for the furtherance of German culture. Most significantly, no doubt in remembrance of his days in Buenos Ayres, Zekki had chosen for this interview the most private room of the Hôtel Moderne, a pension with a bar. where sect could be had; and the worthy representative of the German people, probably nothing loth to have a change from his eternal "Pan-German" diet, accepted his invitation with alacrity. I followed the two gentlemen to make my own investigations, and I certainly got as much amusement, although in a different sense, as one usually does in such haunts. It was really most entertaining to watch Nelken the ex-Jew and Young Turk, with his fez on his head, nodding jovially to all the German officers at the neighbouring tables, and settling the affairs of the realm with this Pan-German representative of the people.

I trust my readers will forgive me if, in spite of the distaste I feel at having to write this unsavoury chapter about German Press representatives and those in high diplomatic authority who commission them, I relate one more episode of a like character before I close. One of these writers employed in the service of the German Embassy had done one of his female employees an injury which cannot be repeated here. His colleague—out of professional jealousy, the other said—gave evidence against him under oath at the German Consulate, and the other brought a charge of perjury against him. The German Consulate, in order not to lose such a trusty champion of the German cause for a trifle like the wounded honour of a mere woman—an Armenian to boot!—simply suppressed the whole case, although all Pera was speaking about it.

Against this we have the case later on of a German journalist, most jealous of German interests, who had a highly important document stolen out of his desk with false keys by one of his clerks in the pay of the Young Turkish Committee. The document was the copy of a very confidential report addressed to high official quarters in Germany, in which there were some rather more uncomplimentary remarks about Enver and Talaat than appeared in the version for public consumption. An Embassy less notoriously cowardly than the German one would simply have shielded their man in consideration of the fact that the report was never meant for publication and of the reprehensible way it had been stolen and made public. But our chicken-hearted diplomats allowed him to be dismissed in disgrace by the Turks, and so practically gave their official sanction to the meanest Oriental methods of espionage.

I have, however, now come to the conclusion from information I have received that German cowardice in this case probably had a background of hypocrisy and malice, for this same journalist had spoken with remarkable freedom, not indeed as a pro-Englander, but in contrast to German and Turkish narrow-mindedness, of how well he had been treated by the English authorities, and particularly General Maxwell in the exercise of his profession in Cairo, where he had been allowed for fully five weeks, after the outbreak of war, to edit a German newspaper. (I have seen the numbers myself and wondered at the almost incredible liberality of the English censorship.) Instead of being sent to Malta he had been treated most fairly and kindly and given every opportunity to get away safely to Syria. Of course the narration of events like these were rather out of place in our "God Punish England" time, and it was no doubt on account of this, apart from all cowardice, that the German Embassy made their fine disstinctions between personal and political morality in the case of their Press representative.

We have spoken of German propaganda for the "Holy War," as carried out by individuals as well as by pamphlets and the Press. The Turkish capital saw a very appreciable amount of this in the shape of wandering adventurers and printed paper. Several thousand Algerian, Tunisian, French West African, Russian Tartar, and Turkestan prisoners of war of Mohammedan religion from the German internment camps were kept for weeks in Pera and urged by the German Government in defiance of all the laws of the peoples to join the "Djihad" against their own rulers.

They were told that they would have the great honour of being presented to the Caliph in Stamboul; as devout Mohammedans they could of course not find much to object to in that. A wonderfully attractive picture was painted for them of the delights of settling in the flourishing lands of the East, and living free of expense instead of starving in prison under the rod of German non-commissioned officers till the far-distant conclusion of peace. One can well imagine how such marvellous conjuring tricks would appeal to these poor fellows.

They have repeatedly told me that they had been promised to be allowed to settle in Turkey without any mention being made of using them again as soldiers. But once on the way to Constantinople there was no further question of asking them what their opinion was of what was being done to them. They were simply treated as Turkish voluntary soldiers and sent off to the Front, to Armenia, and the Irak. How far they were used as real frontline soldiers or in service behind the lines I do not know; what I do know is that they left Constantinople in as great numbers as they came from Germany, armed with rifles and fully equipped for service in the field. One can therefore guess how many of them became "settlers" as they had been promised. Several days running in the early summer of 1916 I saw them being marched off in the direction of the Haidar-Pasha station on the Anatolian Railway. They were headed by a Turkish band, but on not one single face of all these serried ranks did I see the slightest spark of enthusiasm, and the German soldiers and officers escorting each separate section were not exactly calculated to leave the impression with the public that these were zealots fighting voluntarily for their faith who could not get fast enough out to the Front to be shot or hanged by their former masters!

In her system of recruiting in the newly founded kingdom of Poland, Germany demonstrated even more clearly of what she was capable in this direction.

CHAPTER VII

Young Turkish nationalism—One-sided abolition of capitulations— Anti-foreign efforts at emancipation— Abolition of foreign languages— German simplicity —The Turkification of commercial life—Unmistakable intellectual improvement as a result of the war —Trade policy and customs tariff—National production—The founding of new businesses in Turkey—Germany supplanted—German starvation— Capitulations or full European control?—The colonisation and forcible Turkification of Anatolia— "The properties of people who have been dispatched elsewhere"—The "Mohadjirs"—Greek persecutions just before the Great War—The "discovery" of Anatolia, the nucleus of the Ottoman Empire— Turkey finds herself at last—Anatolian dirt and decay— The "Greater Turkey" and the purely Turkish Turkey—Cleavage or concentration?

From the Germans we now turn again to the Turks, to try to fathom tne exact mentality of the Young Turks during the great war, and to discover what were the intellectual sources for their various activities.

To give a better idea of the whole position I will just preface my remarks by stating a few of the outstanding features of the present Young Turkish Government and their dependents. Their first and chief characteristic is hostility to foreigners, but this does not prevent them from making every possible use of their ally Germany, or from appropriating in every walk of life anything European, be it a matter of technical skill, government, civilisation, that they consider might be profitable. Secondly they are possessed of an unbounded store of jingoism, which has its origin in Pan-Turkism with its ruling idea of "Turanism." Pan-Turkism, which seems to be the governing passion of all the leading men of the day, finds expression in two directions. Outwardly it is a constant striving for a "Greater Turkey," a movement that for a large part in its essence, and certainly in its territorial aims, runs parallel with the "Holy War"; inwardly it is a fanatical desire for a general Turkification which finds outlet in political nationalistic measures, some of criminal barbarity, others partaking of the nature of modern reforms, beginning with the language regulations and "internal colonisation" and ending in the Armenian persecutions.

It is worthy of note that of the two intellectual sources of the "Holy War," namely Turanism — which one might reverse and call an extended form of Old-Turkism — and Pan-Islamism, the men of the "Committee for Unity and Progress" have only made logical though unsuccessful use of the former, although theoretically speaking they recognise the value of the latter as well. While Turkish race-fanaticism, which finds practical outlet in Turanistic ideas, is still the intellectual backbone of official Turkey to-day and has to be broken by the present war, the Young Turkish Islam policy is already completely bankrupt and can therefore be studied here dispassionately in all its aspects. We propose to treat the matter in some detail.

All New-Turkish Nationalistic efforts at emancipation had as first principle the abolition of Capitulations. The whole Young Turkish period we have here under review is therefore to be dated from that day, shortly before Turkey's entry into the war, when that injunction was flung overboard which Europe had anxiously placed for the protection of the interests of Europeans on a State but too little civilised. It was Turkey herself that did this after having curtly refused the Entente offer to remove the Capitulations as a reward for Turkey's remaining neutral. Germany, who was equally interested in the existence or non-existence of Capitulations, never mentioned this painful subject to her ally for a very long time, and it was 1916 before she formally recognised the abolition of Capitulations, long after she had lost all hold on Turkey in that direction.

As early as summer 1915 there were clear outward indications in the streets of Constantinople of a smouldering Nationalism ready to break out at any moment. Turkey, under the leadership of Talaat Bey, pursued her course along the well-trodden paths, and the first sphere in which there was evidence of an attempt at forcible Turkification was the language. Somewhere toward the end of 1915 Talaat suddenly ordered the removal of all French and English inscriptions, shop signs, etc., even in the middle of European Pera. In tramcars and at stopping-places the French text was blocked out; boards with public police warnings in French were either removed altogether or replaced by unreadable Turkish scrawls; the street indications were simply abolished. The authorities apparently thought it preferable that the Levantine public should get into the wrong tramcar, should break their legs getting out, pick flowers in the parks and wander round helplessly in a maze of unnamed streets rather than that the spirit of forcible Turkification should make even the least sacrifice to comfort.

Of the thousand inhabitants of Pera, not ten can read Turkish; but under the pressure of the official order and for fear of brutal assault or some kind of underhand treatment in case of non-compliance, the inhabitants really surpassed themselves, and before one could turn, all the names over the shops had been painted over and replaced by wonderful Turkish characters that looked like decorative shields or something of the kind painted in the red and white of the national colours. If one had not noted the entrance to the shop and the look of the window very carefully, one might wander helplessly up and down the Grand Rue de Péra if one wanted to buy something in a particular shop.

But the German, as simple-minded as ever where political matters were concerned, was highly delighted in spite of the extraordinary difficulty of communal life. "Away with French and English," he would shout. "God punish England; hurrah, our Turkish brothers are helping us and favouring the extension of the German language!"

The answer to these pan-German expansion politicians and

language fanatics, whose spiritual home was round the beer-tables of the "Teutonia," was provided by a second decree of Talaat's some weeks later when all German notices had to disappear. A few, who would not believe the order, held out obstinately, and the signs remained in German till they were either supplemented in 1916, on a very clear hint from Stamboul, by the obligatory Turkish language or later quite supplanted. It was not till some time after the German had disappeared—and this is worthy of note—that the Greek signs ceased to exist. Greek had been up to that time the most used tongue and was the commercial language of the Armenians.

Then came the famous language regulations, which even went so far—with a year of grace granted owing to the extraordinary difficulties of the Turkish script—as to decree that in the offices of all trade undertakings of any public interest whatsoever, such as banks, newspapers, transport agencies, etc., the Turkish language should be used exclusively for book-keeping and any written communication with customers. One can imagine the "Osmanic Lloyd" and the "German Bank" with Turkish book-keeping and Turkish letters written to an exclusively European clientèle! Old and trusty employees suddenly found themselves faced with the choice of learning the difficult Turkish script or being turned out in a year's time. The possibility—indeed, the necessity—of employing Turkish hands in European businesses suddenly came within the range of practical politics—and that was exactly what the Turkish Government wanted.

The arrangement had not yet come into operation when I left Constantinople, but it was hanging like the sword of Damocles over commercial undertakings that had hitherto been purely German. Optimists still hoped it never would come to this pass and would have welcomed any political-military blow that would put a damper on Turkey's arrogance. Others, believing firmly in a final Turkish victory, began to learn Turkish feverishly. Be that as it may, the new arrangements were hung up on the walls of all offices in the summer of 1916 and created confusion enough.

80

Many other measures for the systematic Turkification of commercial life and public intercourse followed hard on this first bold step, which I need scarcely mention here. And in spite of the ever-growing number of German officials in the different ministries, partly foisted on the Turkish Government by the German authorities, partly gladly accepted for the moment because the Turks had still much to learn from German organisation and could profit from employing Germans, in spite of the appointment of a number of German professors to the Turkish University of Stamboul (who, however, as a matter of fact, like the German Government officials, had to wear the fez and learn Turkish within a year, and besides roused most unfavourable and anti-German comment in the newspapers), it was soon perfectly evident to every unbiased witness that Germany would find no place in a victorious Turkey after the war if the "Committee for Union and Progress" did not need her. Some sort of light must surely have broken over the last blind optimism of the Germans in the course of the summer of 1916.

Hand in hand with the nationalistic attempt to coerce European businesses into using the Turkish language there went more practical attempts to turkify all the important branches of commerce by the founding of indigenous organisations and the introduction of reforms of more material content than those language decrees. These efforts, in spite of the enormous absorption of all intellectual capabilities and energies in war and the clash of arms, were expressed with a truly marvellous directness of aim, and, from the national standpoint, a truly commendable magnificence of conception.

This latter has indeed never been lacking as a progressive ethnic factor in Turkish politics. The Turks have a wonderful understanding, too, of the importance of social problems, or at least, as a sovereign people, they feel instinctively what in a social connection will further their sovereignty. The war with its enormous intellectual activity has certainly brought all the political and economic resources of the Turks—including the Young Turkish Government—to the highest possible stage of development, and we ought not to be surprised if we often find that measures, whether of a beneficent or injurious character, are not lacking in modern exactness, clever technicality, and thoroughness of conception. Without anticipating, I should just like to note here how this change appears to affect the war. No one can doubt that it will enormously intensify zeal in the fight for the existence of the Turkey of the future, freed from its jingoistic outgrowths, once more come to its senses and confined to its own proper sphere of activity, Anatolia, the core of the Empire. But, on the other hand, iron might and determined warfare against this misguided State are needed to root out false and harmful ideas.

If, after this slight digression, we glance for a moment at the practical measures for a complete Turkification of Turkey, the economic efforts at emancipation and the civic reforms carried through, we find first of all that the new Turkey, when she had thrown the Capitulations overboard, then proceeded to emancipate herself completely from European supervision in the realm of trade and commerce. A very considerable step in advance in the way of Turkish sovereignty and Turkish economic patriotism was the organisation and— since September 1916—execution of the neo-Turkish autonomic custom's tariff, which with one blow gives Turkish finances what the Government formerly managed to extract painfully from the Great Powers bit by bit, by fair means or foul, at intervals of many years, and which with its hard-and-fast scale of taxes—which there appears to be no inclination in political circles at the moment to modify by trade treaties!—means an exceedingly adequate protection of Turkey's national productions, without any reference whatever to the export interests of her allies, and is a very strong inducement to the renaissance of at any rate the most important national industries. The far-flung net of the "Djemiet" (whose acquaintance we have already made in another connection), that purely Turkish commercial undertaking with Talaat Bey at its head, regulating everything as it did, taking everything into its own hands, from the realising of the products of the Anatolian farmers (and incidentally bringing it about that their ally Germany had to pay heavily and always in cash, even although the Government itself owed millions, to Germany and got everything on credit from flour out of Roumania to paper for their journals) to the most difficult rationing of towns, forms a foundation for the nationalising of economic life of the very greatest importance.

The establishment of purely Turkish trade and transport companies, often with pensioned Ministers as directors and principal shareholders, and the new language regulations and other privileges will soon cut the ground away from under the feet of European concerns. Able assistance is given in this direction by the Tanin and the Hilal (the "Crescent"), the newly founded "Committee" paper in the French language (when it is a question of the official influencing of public opinion in European and Levantine quarters, exceptions can be made even in language fanaticism!) in which a series of articles invariably appear at the founding of each new company praising the patriotic zeal of the founders.

Then again there are the increasingly thinly veiled efforts to establish a purely Turkish national banking system. Quite lately there has been a movement in favour of founding a Turkish National Bank with the object of supplanting the much-hated "Deutsche Bank" in spite of the credit it always gives, and that international and preponderatingly French institution, the "Banque Impériale Ottomane," which had already simply been sequestrated without more ado.

The Turks have decided, too, that the mines are to be nationalised, and Turkish companies have already been formed, without capital it is true, to work the mines after the war. The same applies to the railways—in spite of the fine German plans for the Baghdad Railway.

All these wonderful efforts at emancipation are perfectly justified from the patriotic point of view, and are so many blows dealt at Germany, who, quite apart from Rohrbach's Weltpolitik, had at least hoped to find a lucrative field of privileged commercial activity in the country of her close and devoted allies the Turks. It is of supreme significance that while the war is still at its height, while the Empire of the Sultan is defending its very existence at the gates of the capital with German arms and German money, there is manifested with the most startling clearness the failure of German policy, the endangering of all these German "vital interests" in Turkey which according to Pan-German and Imperialistic views were one of the most important stakes to be won by wantonly letting loose this criminal war on Europe.

No doubt many a German was only too well aware of the fact that in this Turkey suddenly roused by the war all the ground had been lost that he had built on with such profit before, and many an anxious face did one see in German circles in Constantinople. I need not tarry here over the drastic comments I heard from so many German merchants on this subject. They show a most curious state of mind on the part of those who had formerly, in their quest for gain and nothing but gain, profited in true parasitical fashion from the financial benefits of the Capitulations and had seen nothing but the money side of this arrangement which was, after all, entered into for other purposes. It was no rare thing and no paradox to find a German company director say, as I heard one say: "If things went against Turkey to-day, I would willingly shoulder my gun, old man as I am."

No thinking man will expend too much grief over the ruthless abolition of the Capitulations, for they were unmoral and gave too much opportunity to parasites and rogues, while they were quite inadequate to protect the interests of civilisation. They may have sufficed in the time of Abdul-Hamid, who was easily frightened off and was always sensible and polite in his dealings with Europe. For the Turkey of Enver and Talaat quite other measures are needed.

One must, according to one's political standpoint, either recognise and accept their nationalistic programme of emancipation or combat it forcibly by introducing full European control. And however willing one may be to let foreign nations develop in their own particular way and work out their own salvation, one's standpoint with regard to a State so behindhand, so fanatical, so misguided as Turkey can be but one: the introduction and continuation at all costs of whatever guarantees the best protection to European civilisation in this land of such importance culturally and historically.

Not only were Europeans, but the natives themselves, affected by the series of measures that one might class together under the heading of Turkish Internal Colonisation and the Nationalising of Anatolia. The programme of the Young Turks was not only a "Greater Turkey," but above all a purely Turkish Turkey; and if the former showed signs of failing because they had over-estimated their powers and their chances in the war or had employed wrong methods, there was nothing at all to hinder a sovereign Government from striving all the more ruthlessly to gain their second point.

The way this Turkification of Anatolia was carried on was certainly not lacking in thoroughness, like all their nationalistic efforts. The best means that lay to hand were the frightful Armenian persecutions which affected a wonderful clearance among the population. "The properties of persons who have been dispatched elsewhere" within the meaning of the Provisory Bill were either distributed free or sold for a mere song to anyone who applied to the Committee for them and proved themselves of the same political persuasion or of pure Turkish or preponderatingly Turkish nationality. The rent was often fixed as low as 30 piastres a month (about 5s. 8d.) for officials and retired military men. In the case of the latter, Enver Pasha thought this an excellent opportunity for getting rid, through the medium of a kindly invitation to settle in the Interior, of those who worried him by their dissatisfaction with his system and who might have prepared difficulties for him. This "settling" was carried out with the greatest zeal in the exceptionally flourishing and fruitful districts of Brussa. Smyrna-Aidin, Eskishehir, Adabazar, Angora, and Adana, where Armenians and Greeks had played such a great, and, to the Turks, unpopular part as pioneers of civilisation.

The semi-official articles in the Tanin were perfectly right in praising the local authorities who in contrast with their former indifference and ignorance "had now fully recognised the great national importance of internal colonisation and the settling of Mohadjirs (emigrants from the lost Turkish territory in Bosnia, Macedonia, Thrace, etc.) in the country." There is nothing to be said in favour of the stupid, unprogressive character of the Anatolian as contrasted with the strength, physical endurance, intelligence, and mobility of these emigrants. The latter had also, generally speaking, lived in more highly developed districts. The great drawback of the Mohadjirs, however, is their instability, their idleness and love of wandering, their frivolity, and their extraordinary fanaticism. As faithful Mohammedans following the standard of their Padishah and leaving the parts of the country that had fallen under Christian rule, they seemed to think they were justified in behaving like spoilt children towards the native population. They treated them with ruthless disregard, they were bumptious, and, if their new neighbours were Greek or Armenian, they inclined to use force, a proceeding which was always possible be cause the Government did not take away their firearms and were even known to have doled them out to stir up unrest. It has occurred more than once that Mohadjirs have crossed swords even with Turkish Anatolians living peacefully in their own villages. One can then easily imagine how much more the heretic giaurs ("Christian dogs," "unclean men") had to suffer at their hands.

I should like to say a word here about these Greek persecutions in Thrace and Western Anatolia that have become notorious throughout the whole of Europe. They took place just before the outbreak of war, and cost thousands of peaceful Greeks—men, women, and children—their lives, and reduced to ashes dozens of flourishing villages and towns. At the time of the murder of Sarajevo, I happened to be staying in the vilajet of Aidin, in Smyrna and the Hinterland, and saw with my own eyes such shameful deeds as must infuriate anyone against the Turkish Government that aids and abets such barbarity—from old women being driven along by a dozen Mohadjirs and dissipated soldiers to the smoking ruins of Phocæa.

Everyone at that time, at any rate in Smyrna, expected the immediate outbreak of a new Græco-Turkish war, and perhaps the only thing that prevented it was the method of procrastination adopted by both sides, for both were waiting for the Dreadnoughts they had ordered, until finally these smaller clouds were swallowed up in the mighty thunder-cloud gathering on the European horizon. Only the extreme speed with which one dramatic event followed another, and my own mobilisation which precluded my writing anything of a political nature, prevented me on that occasion from giving my sinister impressions of Young Turkish jingoism and Mohadjir brutality. Even if I had been able to write what I thought it is extremely doubtful if it would ever have seen the light of day, for the German papers were but little inclined, as I had opportunity of discovering personally, to say anything unpleasant about the Young Turkish Government, whose help they were already reckoning on, and preferred rather to behave in a most un-neutral manner and keep absolutely silent about all the ill-treatment and abuse that had been meted out to Greece. But I remembered these scenes most opportunely later, and that visit of mine to Western Anatolia was certainly most useful in increasing my knowledge of Young Turkish methods of "internal colonisation."

But all the methods used are by no means forcible. Attempts are now being made—and this again is most significant for the spirit of the newest Young Turkish era—to gain a footing in the world of science as opposed to force, and so to be able to carry out their

87

measures more systematically and give them the appearance of beneficent modern social reforms. So it comes about that the Turkish idea of penetrating and "cleaning-up" Anatolia finds practical expression on the one hand in exterminating and robbing the Christian population, while on the other it inclines to efforts which in time may work out to be a real blessing. The common principle underlying both is Nationalism.

Anatolia was suddenly "discovered." At long length the Young Turkish Government, roused intellectually and patriotically by the war and brought to their senses by the terrible loss of human life entailed, suddenly realised the enormous national importance of Anatolia, that hitherto much-neglected nucleus of the Ottoman Empire. Under the spiritual inspiration of Mehmed Emin, the national poet of Anatolian birth whose poems with their sympathy of outlook and noble simplicity of form make such a warm-hearted and successful appeal to the best kind of patriotism, men have begun since 1916, even in the circles of the arrogant "Stambul Effendi," to take an interest in the kaba türk (uncouth Turk), the Anatolian peasant, his needs and his standard of civilisation. The real, needy, primitive Turk of the Interior has suddenly become the general favourite.

A whole series of most remarkable lectures was delivered publicly in the Türk Odjaghi, under the auspices of the Committee, by doctors, social politicians, and political economists, and these were reported and discussed at great length in all the Turkish newspapers. Their subject was the incredible destitution in Anatolia, the devastation wrought by syphilis, malaria, and other terrible dirt diseases, abortions as a result of hopeless poverty, the lack of men as a result of constant military service in many wars, and they called for immediate and drastic reforms.

It is with the greatest pleasure that I acknowledge that this first late step on the way of improvement, this self-knowledge, which appeals to me more thoroughly than anything else I saw in Turkey, is probably really the beginning of a happier era for that beautiful land of Anatolia, so capable of development but so cruelly neglected. For one can no longer doubt that the Government has the real intention of carrying out actual reforms, for they must be only too well aware that the strengthening and healing of Anatolia, the nucleus of the Turkish race, is absolutely essential for any Turkish mastery, and is the very first necessity for the successful carrying out of more far-reaching national exertions. With truly modern realisation of the needs of the case, directly after Dr. Behaeddin Shakir Bey's first compelling lecture, different local government officials, especially the Vali of the Vilajet of Kastamuni, which was notorious for its syphilis epidemics, made unprecedented efforts to improve the terrible hygienic conditions then reigning. Let us hope that such efforts will bear fruit. But this will probably only be the case to any measurable extent later, after the war, when Turkey will find herself really confined to Anatolia, and will have time and strength for positive social work.

In the meantime I cannot get rid of the uneasy impression that this "discovery" of Anatolia and zealous Turkish social politics are no more than a cleverly worked excuse on the part of the Government for further measures of Turkification, and the cloven hoof is unfortunately only too apparent in all this seemingly noble effort on the part of the Committee. One hears and sees daily the methods that go hand in hand with this official pushing into the foreground of the great importance of the purely Turkish elements in Anatolia—Armenian persecutions, trickery, expropriations carried out against Greeks, the yielding up of flourishing districts to quarrelsome Mohadjirs. So long as the Turkish Government fancy themselves conquerors in the great war, so long as they pursue the shadow of a "Greater Turkey," so long as Turkey continues to dissipate her forces she will not accomplish much for Anatolia, in spite of her awakening and her real desire for reform.

Finally, in this discovery of Anatolia, in this desire to put an end to traditional destitution, this recognition of the real import of even the poorest, most primitive, dullest peasant peoples in the undeveloped Interior, so long as they are of Turkish race, in this sudden flood of learned eloquence over the needs and the true inner worth of these miserable neglected Turkish peasants, in this pressing demand for thorough reforms for the economic and social strengthening of this element—measures which with the present ruling spirit of jingoism in the Government threaten to be carried through only at the expense of the non-Turkish population of Anatolia—we see very clear proof that the neo-Turkish movement is a pure race movement, is nothing but Pan-Turkism both outwardly and inwardly, and has very little indeed to do with religious questions or with Islam. The idea of Islam, or rather Pan-Islamism, is a complete failure. This we shall try to show in the following chapter.

CHAPTER VIII

Religion and race—The Islam policy of Abdul-Hamid and of the Young Turks—Turanism and Pan-Islamism as political principles—Turanism and the Quadruple Alliance—Greed and race-fanaticism— Religious traditions and modern reforms—Reform in the law—A modern Sheikh-ul-Islam—Reform and nationalisation—The Armenian and Greek Patriarchates—The failure of Pan-Islamism—The alienation of the Arabs—Djemal Pasha's "hangman's policy" in Syria—Djemal as a "Pro-French"— Djemal and Enver—Djemal and Germany—His true character—The attempt against the Suez Canal—Djemal's murderous work nears completion— The great Arabian and Syrian Separatist movement —The defection of the Emir of Mecca and the great Arabian catastrophe.

In little-informed circles in Europe people are still under the false impression that the Young Turks of to-day, the intellectual and political leaders of Turkey in this war, are authentic, zealous, and even fanatical Mohammedans, and superficial observers explain all unpleasant occurrences and outbreaks of Young Turkish jingoism on Pan-Islamic grounds, especially as Turkey has not been slow in proclaiming her "Holy War." But this conception is entirely wrong. The artificial character of the "Djihad," which was only set in motion against a portion of the "unbelievers," while the others became more and more the ruling body in Turkey, is the best proof of the untenability of this theory. The truth is that the present political regime is the complete denial of the Pan-Islamic idea and the substitution of the Pan-Turkish idea of race.

Abdul-Hamid, that much-maligned and dethroned Sultan, who, however, towers head and shoulders above all the Young Turks put together in practical intelligence and statesmanly skill, and would never have committed the unpardonable error of throwing in his lot with Germany in the war and so bringing about the certain downfall of Turkey, was the last ruler of Turkey that knew how to make use of Pan-Islamism as a successful instrument of authority. Enver and Talaat and all that breed of jingoists on the Ittahad (Committee for Union and Progress) were upstarts without any schooling in political history, and so all the more inclined to the doctrinal revolutionism and short-sighted fanaticism of the successful adventurer, and were much too limited to recognise the tremendous political import of Pan-Islamism. Naturally once they had conceived the idea of the "Djihad," they tried to make theoretical use of Pan-Islamism; but practically, far from extending Turkey's influence to distant Arabian lands, to the Soudan and India, they simply let Turkey go to ruin through their Pan-Turkish illusions and their race-fanaticism.

Abdul-Hamid with his clever diplomacy managed to maintain, if not the real sympathies, at any rate the formal loyalty of the Arabs and their solidarity with the rest of the Ottoman Empire. It was he who conceived the idea of that undertaking of eminent political importance, the Hedjaz Railway, which facilitates pilgrimages to the holy cities of Mecca and Medina and links up the Arabian territory with the Turkish, and he was always able to quell any disturbances in these outlying parts of the Empire with very few troops indeed. Nowadays the Young Turkish Government, even if they had the troops to spare, might send a whole army to the Hedjaz and they would be like an island of sand in the midst of that stormy Arab sea. The Arabs, intellectually far superior to the Turks, have at last made up their minds to defy their oppressors, and all the Arabic-speaking parts of the Ottoman Empire may be taken as already lost, no matter what the final result of the great war may be.

The Young Turks had scarcely come into power when they began with incredible lack of tact to treat the Arabs in a most supercilious manner, although as a matter of fact the Arabs far surpassed them in intellect and culture. They inaugurated a most un-modern campaign of shameless blood-sucking, cheated them of their rights, treated them in a bureaucratic manner, and generally acted in such an unskilful way that they finally alienated for ever the Arab element as they had already done in the case of the Armenians, the Greeks, and the Albanians.

The ever-recurring disturbances in Yemen, finally somewhat inadequately quelled by Izzet Pasha, are still in the memory of all. And later, directly after the reconquering of Adrianople during the Second Balkan war, there was another moment of real national rebirth when a reconciliation might have been effected. The visit of a great Syrian and Arabian deputation to the Sultan to congratulate him over this auspicious event should have provided an excellent opportunity. I was staying some months then in Constantinople on my way back from Africa, and I certainly thought that the half-broken threads might have been knotted together again then if the Young Turks had only approached the Arabs in the right way. Even the great Franco-British attack on Stamboul might have been calculated to rouse a feeling of solidarity among the Mohammedans living under the Ottoman flag, and in the autumn and winter of 1915-1916 Arab troops actually did defend the entrance to the Dardanelles with great courage and skill. But Arab loyalty could not withstand for ever the mighty flood of race-selfishness that possessed the Young Turks right from the moment of their entry into the war. The enthusiasm of the Arabs soon disappeared when Pan-Turkish ideas were proclaimed all too clearly even to the inhabitants of their own land, when an era of systematic enmity towards the non-Turkish parts of the population was introduced and the heavy fist of the Central Committee was laid on the southern parts of the Empire as well.

An attempt was made to bring the ethnic principle of "Turanism" within the region of practical politics, but it simply degenerated into complete race-partiality and was not calculated to further the ideas of Pan-Islamism and the Turko-Arabian alliance which were both of such importance in the present war. It is this idea of Turanism that lies at the back of the efforts being made towards a purely Turkish Turkey, and that of course makes it clear at once that it must to a very large extent oppose the idea of Pan-Islamism. It is true that both principles may be made use of side by side as sources of propaganda for the idea of expansion and the policy of a "Greater Turkey." Turanists peep over the crest of the Caucasus down into the Steppes of the Volga where the Russian Tartars live, and to the borders of Western Siberia and Inner China where in Russian Turkestan a race of people of very close kinship live and where very probably the Ottoman people had their cradle. The Pan-Islamists want the alliance of these Russian parts as well, but from another point of view, and, above all, they aim at the expansion of Ottoman rule to the farthest corners of Africa and South-West Asia, to the borders of negro territory, and through Persia, Afghanistan, and Baluchistan to the foot of the Himalayas, while on grounds of practical politics they strive to abolish the old, seemingly insurmountable antithesis between Sonnites and Shiites within the sanctuary of Islam.

The programme of the so-called "Djihad" works on this principle, but goes much farther. As well as stirring up against their present rulers those parts of Egypt and Tripoli which once owned allegiance to the Sultan and the Atlas lands, which are at any rate spiritually dependent on the Caliph in Stamboul, the "Djihad" aims at introducing the spirit of independence into all English, French, Italian, and Russian Colonial territory by rousing the Mohammedans and so doing infinite harm to the enemies of Turkey. It is most important, therefore, always to differentiate between this "Holy War" "stirring-up" propaganda from Senegal to Turkestan and British India, and the more territorial Pan-Islamism of the present war, which goes hand in hand with the efforts being made towards a "Greater Turkey." Instead of uniting all these principles skilfully for the realisation of a great end, making sure of the Arab element by wisely restraining their selfish and exaggeratedly pro-Turkish instincts and their despotic lust for power, and so giving their programme of expansion southwards some prospect of succeeding, the Turks gave way right from the beginning of the war to such a flood of brutal, narrow-minded race-fanaticism and desire to enrich the Turkish element at the cost of the other inhabitants of the country, that no one can really be surprised at the pitiable result of the efforts to secure a Greater Turkey.

I should just like to give one small example of the fanatical hatred that exists even in high official circles against the non-Turkish element in this country of mixed race. The following anecdote will give a clear enough idea of the ruling spirit of fanaticism and greed. I was house-hunting in Pera once and could not find anything suitable. I approached a member of the Committee and he said in solemn earnest: "Oh, just wait a few weeks. We are all hoping that Greece will declare war on us before long, and then all the Greeks will be treated as the Armenians have been. I can let you have the nicest villa on the Bosporus. But then," he added with gleaming eyes, "we won't be so stupid as merely to turn them out. These Greek dogs (köpek rum) will have the pleasure of seeing us take everything away from them—everything—and compelling them to give up their own property by formal contract."

I can guarantee that this is practically a word-for-word rendering of this extraordinary outburst of fanaticism and greed on the part of an otherwise harmless and decent man. I could not help shuddering at such opinions. Apparently it was not enough that Turkey was already at war with three Great Powers; she must needs seek armed conflict with Greece, so that, as was the outspoken, the open, and freely-admitted intention of official persons, she might then deal with four and a half millions of Ottoman Greeks, practically her own countrymen, as she had done with the unfortunate Armenians. In face of such opinions one cannot but realise how unsure the existence of the Young Turkish State has become by its entry into the war, and cannot but foresee that this race-fanaticism will lead the nation to political and social suicide. Can one imagine a purely Turkish Turkey, when even the notion of a Greater Turkey failed?

Pessimists have often said of the Turkish question that the Turks' principal aim in determining on a complete Turkification of Anatolia by any, even the most brutal, means, is that at the conclusion of war they can at least say with justification: "Anatolia is a purely Turkish country and must therefore be left to us." What they propose to bequeath to the victorious Russians is an Armenia without Armenians!

The idea of "Turanism" is a most interesting one, and as a widespread nationalistic principle has given much food for thought to Turkey's ally, Germany. Turanism is the realisation, reawakened by neo-Turkish efforts atpolitical and territorial expansion, of the original race-kinship existing between the Turks and the many pe oples inhabiting the regions north of the Caucasus, between the Volga and the borders of Inner China, and particularly in Russian Central Asia. Ethnographically this idea was perfectly justified, but politically it entails a tremendous dissipation of strength which must in the end lead to grave disappointment and failure. All the Turkish attempts to rouse up the population of the Caucasus either fell on unfruitful ground or went to pieces against the strong Russian power reigning there. Enver's marvellous conception of an offensive against Russian Transcaucasia led right at the beginning of the war to terrible bloodshed and defeat.

People in neutral countries have had plenty of opportunity of judging of the value of those arguments advanced by Tatar professors and journalists of Russian citizenship for the "Greater-Turkish" solution of the race questions of the Russian Tatars and Turkestan, for these refugees from Baku and the Caucasus, paid by the Stamboul Committee, journeyed half over Europe on their propaganda tour. The idea of Turanism has been taken up with such enthusiasm by the men of the Young Turkish Committee, and utilised with such effect for purposes of propaganda and to form a scientific basis for their neo-Turkish aims and aspirations, that a stream of feeling in favour of the Magyars has set in in Turkey, which has not failed to demolish to a still greater extent their already weakened enthusiasm for their German allies. And it is not confined to purely intellectual and cultural spheres, but takes practical form by the Turks declaring, as they have so often done in their papers in almost anti-German articles about Turanism, that what they really require in the way of European technique or European help they much prefer to accept from their kinsmen the Hungarians rather than from the Germans.

To the great annoyance of Germany, who would like to keep her heavy hand laid on the ally whom she has so far guided and for whom she pays, the practical results of the idea of Turanism are already noticeable in many branches of economic and commercial life. The Hungarians are closely allied to the Turks not only by blood but in general outlook, and form a marked contrast to Germany's cold and methodical calculation in worming her way into Turkish commercial life. After the war when Turkey is seeking for stimulation, it will be easy enough to make use of Hungarian influence to the detriment of Germany. Turanistic ideas have even been brought into play to establish still more firmly the union between Turkey and her former enemy Bulgaria, and the people of Turkey are reminded that the Bulgars are not really Slavs but Slavic Fino-Tartars.

In proportion as the Young Turks have brought racial politics to a fine art, so they have neglected the other, the religious side. More and more, Islam, the rock of Empire, has been sacrificed to the needs of race-politics. Those who look upon Enver and Talaat and their consorts to-day as a freemasonry of timeserving opportunists rather than as good Mohammedans come far nearer the truth than those who believe the idea spread by ignorant globe-trotters that every Turk is a zealous follower of Islam. It was not for nothing that Enver Pasha, the adventurer and revolutionary, went so far even in externals as to arouse the stern disapproval of a wide circle of his people. With true time-serving adaptability to all modern progress—and who will blame him?—he even finally sacrificed the Turkish soldier's hallowed traditional headgear, the fez. While the kalpak, even in its laced variety, could still be called a kind of field-grey or variegated or fur edition of the fez, the ragged-looking kabalak called the "Enveriak" to distinguish it from other varieties, is certainly on the way towards being a real sun helmet. Still more recently (summer 1916) a black-and-white cap that looks absolutely European was introduced into the Ottoman Navy. The simple, devout Mohammedan folk were most unwilling to accept these changes which flew direct in the face of all tradition. They may be externals of but little importance, but in spite of their insignificance they show clearly the ruling spirit in official Young Turkish spheres.

This is in the harmless realm of fashion, or at any rate military fashion, exactly the same spirit as has caused the Turkish Government to undertake since 1916 radical changes in the very much more important field of private and public law. Special commissions consisting of eminent Turkish lawyers have been formed to carry through this reform of law and justice, and they have been hard at work ever since their formation. What is characteristic and modern about the reform is that the preponderating rôle hitherto played by the Sheriat Law, founded on the Koran and at any rate semi-religious, is to be drastically curtailed in favour of a system of purely Civil law, which has been strung together from the most varied sources, even European law being brought under contribution, and the "Code Napoléon," which has hitherto only been used in Commercial law. This of course leads to a great curtailment of the activity and influence of the kadis and muftis, the semi-religious judges, who have now to yield place to a more mundane system. The first inexorable consequence of the reform was that the Sheikh-ul-Islam, the highest authority of Islam in the whole Ottoman Empire, had to give up a large part of his powers, and incidentally of his income.

The changes made were so far-reaching, and the spirit of the reform so modern, that, in spite of the unshakable power of Talaat's truly dictatorial Cabinet which got it passed, a concession had to be made to the public opinion roused against the measure. The form was kept as it was, but the Sheikh-ul-Islam, Haïri Effendi, refused ostensibly to sign the decree and gave in his resignation. Not only, however, was an immediate successor found for him (Mussa Kiazim Effendi), who gave his signature and even began to work hard for the reform, but—and this is most significant for the relationship of the Young Turks towards Islam—Haïri Effendi, the same ex-Sheikh-ul-Islam who had proclaimed the Fetwa for the "Holy War," gave up his post without a murmur, and in the most peaceable way, and remained one of the principal pillars of the "Committee for Union and Progress." His resignation was nothing but a farce to throw dust in the eyes of the all-too-trusting lower classes. After he had succeeded by this manoeuvre in getting the reform of the law (which as a measure of Turkification was of more consequence to him now than his own sadly curtailed juristic functions) accepted at a pinch by the conservative population who still clung firmly to Islam, he went on to play his great role in the programme of jingoism. A "measure of Turkification" we called it, for that is what it amounts to practically, like everything else the men of the "Ittihad" take in hand.

I tried to give some hint of this within the limits of the censorship as long ago as the summer of 1916 in a series of articles I wrote for the Kölnische Zeitung. Here I should like just to confine myself to one point. Naturally the reform of the law aimed principally at substituting these newly formed pure Turkish conceptions for the Arabian legal ideas that had been the only thing available hitherto. (Everything that this victorious Turkey had absorbed and worked up in the way of civilised notions was either Arabian or Persian or of European origin.) It set to work now in the sphere of family law, which hitherto had been specially sacrosanct and only subordinate to the religious Sheria, and where tradition was strongest—not like commercial and maritime law which had been quite modern for a long time.

The reform went so far that it even tried to introduce a kind of civil

99

marriage, whereas up till now all marriages, divorces, and everything to do with inheritance had taken place exclusively before religious officials. I may just add that these newest reforms give women no wider rights than they had before. Perhaps this may be taken as an indication that they have been conceived far less from a social than from a political point of view. What induced the Turkish Government to introduce anything so entirely modern as civil marriage in defiance of age-old custom was more than likely the desire to put an end to non-Turkish Ottomans contracting marriages and making arrangements about inheritance, etc., before their own privileged, ethnically independent organisations, and so to deal the final death-blow to the Armenian and Greek Patriarchates. If Family Law was modernised in this way, there would not be the faintest shadow of excuse left for the existence of these institutions which enjoyed a far-reaching and influential autonomy.

The Armenian Patriarchate got short shrift indeed. By dissolving the Patriarchate in the Capital, breaking off all relations with the Armenian headquarters in Etzmiadjin and allowing only a very small remainder of Patriarchate to be sent up in Jersusalem under special State supervision, the Turks, as a logical sequence to the Armenian atrocities, simply dealt the death-blow in the summer of 1916 to this important social institution.

The Greek organisation, however, conducted by a more numerous and, outwardly at any rate, better protected people, offered far more resistance, and could not be simply wiped out with a stroke of the pen. A direct attempt to suppress it was made as early as 1910, but broke down entirely in face of the firm attitude of the Greek Patriarch in Constantinople. Now the Young Turks seem to have come to the conclusion that less drastic methods, beginning on a juristic basis, may have a better effect.

We have taken this one example in order to get at the whole neo-Turkish method of procedure. It consists in pushing forward, if need be with greater delicacy than before and on the round-about road of real modern reforms, towards the one immovable goal: the complete Turkification of Turkey. The reform of the law, which we have treated more exhaustively as an example of the first rank, is typical of the Young Turkish national tendency. Naturally it has its use, too, as a means of further throwing off the foreign political yoke. Through the modernising of the whole Turkish legal system, Europe is to be shown that the Capitulations can be dispensed with.

The reform throws a vivid light, too, on the inner relationship of the jingoistic, pure Pan-Turkish leaders of present-day Turkey towards religion. And it is perhaps not generally known that at all the deliberations of the "Committee" where the will of Talaat, the uncrowned king of Turkey, is alone decisive, the opinion of the Grand Master of the Turkish Freemasons is always listened to, and that he is one of the most willing tools of the "Ittihad."

No, the members of the "Committee for Union and Progress" have for a very long time simply snapped their fingers at Islam if it hindered them making use of and profiting from their own subjects. They know very well how to retain at least the outward semblance of friendliness so long as Islam does not directly cross the path of Pan-Turkism. But the Armenian atrocities, instigated by Talaat, have as little to do with religion, they are as exclusively the result of pure race-fanaticism, professional jealousy, and greed, as the hostile, devil-may-care attitude towards Greece, and the millions of well-to-do Ottoman Greeks who are the next troublesome competitors and suitable victims of aggrandisement to be disposed of after the Armenians, or as the terrible persecutions against the highest class of Syrians and Arabs pictured in Djemal Pasha's famous paper. They are Turks, pure Turks with the most narrow-minded jingoistic point of view, and not broad-minded Mohammedans, that sit on the Committee in "Nur-el-Osmanieh" in Stamboul and make all these wonderful political plans, from internal reforms and measures of government which attempt to adapt themselves to European technique by sacrificing ancient

101

traditions, to the hangman's tactics employed against their own subjects.

Take the case of the Syrians and the Arabs. The "Ittihad" clique, weltering in a fog of Pan-Turkish illusion, were yet not without anxiety with regard to the intellectual and social superiority, to say nothing of the political sharpness, of these peoples compared with the Turks. They had yielded entirely to their brutal instincts of extermination and suppression towards foreign races, and the Germans had made no attempt to curb them. They were political parvenus suddenly freed from the control of the civilised Great Powers, and they did not know how to make use of that freedom. Perhaps they felt themselves already on the edge of an abyss and were constrained to snatch what they could while there was yet time.

Is it any wonder, then, that the Turks should throw over all trace of decency towards the Syrians and the Arabs once they were sure that these peoples, who regarded their oppressors with most justifiable hatred, would refuse to have anything to do with the "Holy War" of the Turanian Pseudo-Caliph?

The last remnants of the traditional Pan-Islamic esteem of their Arab neighbours, already sadly shattered by the Young Turks' ruthless policy towards them since 1909, were flung light-heartedly overboard by a Government that knew they were to blame for the Arab defection but thought they had found a substitute that appealed more to their true Asiatic character in these Turanistic dreams of expansion and measures of Turkification. And while fanatical adventurers and money-grubbing deputies paid by the easily duped German Embassy were preaching a perfectly useless "Holy War" on the confines of the Arabian territory of the Turkish Empire, towards the part occupied by the English, while Enver Pasha continued to visit the holy places of Islam, where he got a frosty enough reception, although the wonderfully worded communiques on the subject succeeded in blinding the population to the true state of affairs, "the hangman's policy" of Djemal Pasha, the Commander of the Fourth Osmanic Army, and Naval Minister, had been for a long time in full swing in the old civilised land of Syria against the best families among the Mohammedan as well as the Christian population. The whole civilised world is laying up a store of accusations of this kind against the Turks, and it is to be hoped that a public sentence will be passed on these gentlemen of the "Ittihad" on the conclusion of peace by a combined court of Europeans and Americans.

Here again the Young Turkish Government assumed the existence of a widespread conspiracy and a Syrian and Arabian Separatist movement towards autonomy, which was to free these lands from Turkish rule and to be established under Anglo-French protection. At the time of the Armenian persecutions the Committee had managed most cunningly to turn the whole Armenian question to their own account by publishing false official reports by the thousand, accompanied by any number of photographs of "bands of conspirators," the authenticity of which never has been proved and never will be; indeed one can only wonder where the Turkish Government got them from.

In this case again there was no lack of official printed commentaries on Djemal Pasha's "hanging list," and any reader of the Journal de Beyrouth in war-time would have had no difficulty in compiling it. It is certainly not my intention to question the existence of a Separatist movement towards autonomy in Syria, but it was a sporadic tendency only, and ought never to have been made the excuse for the wholesale execution of highly respected and well-born citizens who had nothing whatever to do with the matter.

In the Young Turkish memorandum on this act of spying and bloodshed, the passages most underlined and printed in the boldest characters, the passages which, according to official intention, were to justify these frightful reprisals, form the most terrible indictment ever brought against Turkish despotism, and provide the most complete proof of the truth of all the accusations made against the Turkish Government by the ill-treated and oppressed Syrians and Arabians. On anyone who does not read with Young Turkish eyes the memorandum makes directly the opposite impression to what was intended. And even if the Separatist movement had existed in any greater extent—which was quite out of the question owing to lack of weapons, conflicting interests, the contrasts in the people themselves, some of them Mohammedan, some Christian, some sectarian, and the impossibility of any kind of organisation under the stern discipline of Turkish rule—the Turks would have most richly deserved it and it would have been justified by the thousands of brutalities inflicted by the Old and Young Turkish regimes on the highly civilised Arabian people and their industrious and commercial neighbours the Syrians, who had always been much influenced by European culture. Anyone who has once watched how the Committee in Stamboul made a pretext of events on the borders of Caucasia to exterminate a whole people, including women and children, even in Western and Central Anatolia and the Capital, can no longer be in the least doubt as to the methods employed by Djemal Pasha, the "hangman" of Syrians and Arabs, how grossly he must have exaggerated and misstated the facts to find enough victims so that he could look on for a year and a half with a cigar in his mouth—as he himself boasted—while the flower of Syrian and Arabian youth, the élite of society, and the aged heads of the best families in the land were either hanged or shot.

I should like to take the opportunity here of giving a short description of Djemal Pasha, this man who, according to Turkish ideas, is destined still to play a great part in Turkish politics. I should also like to clear up a misunderstanding that seems to exist in civilised Europe with regard to him. There is still an idea abroad that Djemal Pasha is pro-French, this man who set out on his adventure against the Suez Canal as "Vice-king of Egypt," and, after he had been beaten there, settled in Syria as dictator with unlimited power—even openly defying the Central Government in Constantinople when he felt piqued—so that as commander of the

Fourth Army he could support the attempt against Egypt, but principally to satisfy his murderous instincts. Anyone who has seen this man close at hand (whom a German journalist belonging to the Berliner Tageblatt with the most fulsome flattery once called one of the handsomest men in Turkey) knows enough. Small, thickset, a beard and a pair of cunning cruel eyes are the most prominent features of this face from which everyone must turn in disgust who remembers the "hangman's" part played by the man.

It is extraordinary that he should still pass as Pro-French in many quarters, and perhaps it is part of his slyness to preserve this rôle. Djemal is not Pro-French; he is only the most calculating of all the leading men of Turkey.

He certainly had pro-French tendencies, in the current meaning of the word, before the war; that is, he thought the interests of his country would be best safeguarded against German machinations for winning over the Young Turks by taking advantage of Turkey's traditional friendship for France. He was also against Turkey's participation in the war on the side of the Central Powers, and he was furiously angry when the fleet which was supposed to be under his control appeared against his will under the direction of the German Admiral of the Goeben and Breslau in the Black Sea.

But when the war actually broke out, he very soon accommodated himself to the new state of affairs. Instead of handing in his resignation, he added to his naval duties the chief command of the army operating against Egypt, for Djemal's chief characteristics were characterless opportunism and inordinate ambition. Suiting his opinions to the facts of the case, he was not long in advertising his Pro-French feelings again so that he might be popular with the people of Syria. That of course did not prevent him later on from carrying out his "hangman's policy" against the Syrians who were bound by so many social ties to France. From that it is not difficult to judge just how genuine his Pro-French feelings are!

The only genuine thing in his whole attitude is his admitted deep hatred of Germany and his personal animosity towards the pro-German Enver Pasha, arising partly from jealousy, partly from a feeling of being slighted, and only concealed for appearance' sake. During the war he has often enough made very plain utterances of his hatred of Germany, and it would certainly betoken ill for German politics in Turkey if Djemal Pasha succeeded in obtaining a more active rôle in the Central Government. So far the Minister for War has managed to hold him at arm's length, and Djemal has no doubt found it of advantage to wait for a later moment, and content himself for the present with his actual powerful position.

From his own repeated anti-German speeches it has, however, been only too easy to glean that his anti-German opinions and actions are not the result of his being Pro-French, but of his being a jingoistic Pan-Turk. He may simulate Pro-French feelings again and play them as the trump card in his surely approaching decisive struggle with Enver Pasha, when Enver's system has failed; Djemal will no doubt maintain then that he foresaw everything, and that he has always been for France and the Entente. Everyone who knows his character is at any rate sure of one thing, and that is that he will stop at nothing, even a rising against the Central Government, if his ambitious opportunism should so dictate it. It is to be hoped, however, that public opinion among the Entente will not be deceived as to his true character, and will recognise that he is nothing more than a jingoistic, greedy, raging Young Turkish fanatic and one of the most cunning at that. It would really be doing too much honour to a man with a murderer's face and a murderer's instinct to credit him with honest sympathies for France.

Djemal's work is nearing fruition. His cruel executions, his cynical breaking of promises in Syria, have at any rate contributed, along with other politically more important tendencies which have been cleverly utilised by England for the establishment of an Arabian Caliphate, towards the decisive result that the Emir of Mecca has revolted against the Turks. The Emir's son and his great Arabian suite had to pay a prolonged visit to Djemal at one time, and it is evident that the brutal execution of Arabian notables that he saw then directly influenced his father's attitude. The movement is bound to spread, and slowly and surely it will roll on till it ends in the full and perfect separation from Turkey of all Arabic-speaking districts as far as Northern Syria and the borders of Southern Kurdistan. The so-called Separatist movement, that Djemal tried to drown in a sea of blood before it was well begun, is now an actual fact.

In Egypt England has been seeing for quite a long time the practical and favourable results of her success in founding the Arabian Caliphate. She has now gained practically absolute security for her rule on the Nile, and she has even been able to remove troops and artillery from the Suez Canal to other fronts. The German dream of an offensive against Egypt vanished long ago; now even the last trace of a German-Turkish attempt against the Canal has ceased, and the English troops have moved the scene of their operations to Southern Palestine. While I write these lines, there comes from the other side, from Arabian Mesopotamia, the news of the recapture of Kut-el-Amara by British troops. I should not like to prophesy what moral or political results the fall of Baghdad, Medina, and Jerusalem will have for Turkish rule; possibly, nay probably, iron necessity, the impossibility of returning, the constraint imposed by their German Allies—for Turkey is fully under German military rule—may weaken the direct results of even such catastrophes as these. But the hearts which beat to-day with high hopes for the freedom of Great Arabia and autonomy for Syria under Franco-English protection will flame with new rapture, and in the Turkish capital all grades of society will realise that Osmanic power is on the decline.

Meantime Djemal Pasha is still occupied in Syria raking in the property of the murdered citizens and dividing it up among his minions, the least very often being given over to commissions consisting of individuals of extremely doubtful reputation. When he is not thus busily engaged, he spends his time round the green table playing poker. It is to be ardently hoped that even this great organiser will soon be at the end of his tether in Syria and have to leave the country where he has kinged in royally for two years. Then, perhaps, the moment may come when things are going so badly for the whole of Turkey that Djemal will at last have the opportunity, in spite of the failure of his policy in Syria, of measuring his military strength against his hated enemy Enver in Stamboul. That would be the beginning of the last stage before the complete collapse of Turkey.

CHAPTER IX

Anti-war and pro-Entente feelings among the Turks— Turkish pessimism about the war—How would Abdul-Hamid have acted?—A war of prevention against Russia—Russia and a neutral Turkey— The agreement about the Dardanelles—A peaceful solution scorned—Alleged criminal intentions on the part of the Entente; the example of Greece and Salonika—To be or not to be?—German influence— Turkey stakes on the wrong card—The results.

There has been no lack of cross currents against the war policy of the Young Turkish Government. Ever since the entry of Turkey into the war, there has been a deeply rooted and unshakeable conviction among all kinds and conditions of men, even in the circles of the Pashas and the Court—the people of Turkey take too little interest in politics and are composed of far too heterogeneous elements for there to be anything in the nature of what we call "public opinion"—that Turkey's alliance with the Central Powers was a complete mistake and that it can lead to no good. It is of course known that since the outbreak of war Turkey has not only been under martial law and in a state of siege, but that under the regime of a brutal military dictatorship, with its system of espionage, personal liberty has been practically null and void. Any expressions of disapproval, therefore, or agitations against the "committee" are naturally only possible in most intimate circles, and that with all secrecy. Little or nothing of the true opinions of this or that personage ever trickles through to publicity, and so it is utterly impossible, except from quite detached symptoms, to get any proper idea of what are the real thoughts and feelings of those cultured Turks who do not belong to the "Ittihad" and have no part in their system of pillage and aggrandisement.

In spite of the limited information available it will be worth while, I think, to go into these counter-streams a little more fully. In pretty well every grade of society and among all nationalities in Turkey, there is the conviction that the old Sultan Abdul-Hamid would never have committed the fateful error of declaring war against the Entente and binding himself hand and foot to Germany. In the case of Turkey's remaining neutral, the Entente had formally promised her territorial integrity; Turkey refused. She felt herself driven to a war of prevention, principally through fear of the power of Russia. The statements made by those who agreed with Enver and Pasha and pushed for the war, that Turkey in the case of non-participation would be completely thrown on the mercy of a victorious Russia and that Russia's true aim in the war was the Dardanelles and Constantinople, have never been authenticated. There are still Turks, anti-Russian Turks, who even admitted this possibility, and yet believed the word of the Entente—at any rate of the Western Powers— and trusted to England's throwing her weight into the scale against Russia's plans of conquest, if Turkey remained neutral. They saw and still see no necessity for the Turkish Government to have entered on a war of prevention.

Russia's aim was the Straits and Constantinople—well and good. But Russia would by hook or by crook have had to come to a friendly agreement with Turkey and could not have simply broken a definite promise given by the combined Entente to Turkey. It would have been quite different if Russia had demanded Constantinople from the Western Powers as the price of her participation in the war against Germany; then, but only then, the Entente would perhaps have had to come to an agreement satisfying Russia on this head. But Russia had quite other ideas, and long before Turkey's entry into the war and without any prospects of getting Constantinople, she flung her whole weight against Germany and Austria right at the beginning of the war.

The treaty with regard to Constantinople between the Western Powers and Russia was not signed till six months after Turkey declared war, and England would certainly never have allowed Russia to encroach on a really neutral or sympathetically neutral

Turkey. Then, but only then, there might have been some foundation in fact for the ideas one heard advanced by German-Turkish illusionists who would still have liked to believe that there was continual dissension within the Entente, even long after the official notification of the Anglo-Russian treaty with regard to the Straits, and by some even after the speech of the Russian minister Trepoff, that the English occupation of the islands at the entrance to the Dardanelles, which could be made into a second Gibraltar, aimed chiefly at blocking the Straits and preventing Russia from gaining undisturbed possession of Constantinople. Specially optimistic people even look to that chimerical antagonism between Russia and England for the salvation of Turkey, should Germany be finally overcome.

Whether she liked it or not, then, Russia would have had to come to a friendly agreement with Turkey, had the latter remained neutral, in order to gain the desired goal. And this goal would have been necessarily limited, by the fact of Turkey's non-entry on the enemy side, rather to the stoppage of German Berlin-Baghdad efforts at expansion, the prevention of any strangulation of the enormous Russian trade in the south and desperate opposition to any attempt to keep Russia away from the Mediterranean, than to an attack on Turkey and her vital interests. And who knows whether under such an agreement, bound as it was to give Russia certain liberties and privileges in the Straits, Turkey also might not have got much in exchange, at any rate on financial lines, and might not also have obtained permission at last to develop Armenia by that west-to-east railway so long desired by the Turks and so strongly opposed by the Russians ?

Would the terrible bloodshed in the present war, the complete economic exhaustion entailed, and the risk of a doubtful outcome of the fight for existence or non-existence not have been far outweighed by the prospect, in the case of a friendly agreement with Russia, of seeing the orthodox cross again planted on the Hagia Sophia, an international régime established in

Constantinople—with certain Russian privileges and the satisfaction of certain Russian moral demands, it is true, but otherwise nothing to disturb Turkish life in Stamboul or in any way prejudice Turkish prestige? Even the prospect of having to raze the forts on the Straits to the ground in order to give free access from the Mediterranean, or the necessity of having to inaugurate a more humane and beneficent policy in Armenia, perhaps with European supervision over the carrying out of the reforms would surely have been preferable to the present state of affairs. These would all have ensured for Turkey a long period of peace, capital wealth and intellectual and social improvement, perhaps at the expense of a momentary hurt to her feelings,—but these had been far more severely wounded already, as, for example, when she had to look on helplessly while bit after bit of her Empire was torn from her. It would have been impossible for Russia to get more than this from Turkey had she remained neutral. Her sovereignty and territorial integrity would have been completely guaranteed.

But Turkey thought she had to stake all, her whole existence, on one card, and she staked on the wrong one, as is recognised now by thousands of intelligent Turks. Believers in the war policy followed by the Government make themselves hoarse maintaining that if Russia had not gradually overpowered a neutral Turkey to win Constantinople completely, at any rate the Entente would have finally forced her to join their side; in either case, therefore, war was inevitable. They point to Salonika, and, in face of all reason, maintain that the Entente Powers would in all probability have treated Turkey exactly as they treated Greece. They forget that their geographical position is entirely different, and would have a very different effect on military tactics. If Turkey had remained a sympathetic neutral, so would Bulgaria; or else the whole of the Balkan States, from Roumania and Bulgaria to Greece, would have joined the Entente right at the beginning. In either case there would have been no necessity at all for Turkey to join, for what military obligations had she to fulfil? The Entente would certainly never have driven Turkey to fight, simply to get the benefit of the Turkish soldiers available; there is no truth whatever in the statements circulated about unscrupulous compulsion with this end in view.

The benefit for the Entente of Turkey's sympathetic neutrality would have been so enormous that they would most certainly have been content with that. Neither in Germany nor in Turkey is there any doubt whatever in military circles that it was Turkey's entry into the war on the German side and her blocking of the Straits, and so preventing Russia from obtaining supplies of ammunition and other war material, that has so far saved the Central Powers. Had Turkey remained neutral, constant streams of ammunition would have poured into Russia, Mackensen's offensive would have had no prospect at all of success, and Germany would have been beaten to all intents and purposes in 1915. The Turks do not scruple to let Germany feel that this is so on every suitable or unsuitable occasion.

The Entente would certainly never have moved a finger to disturb Turkey's sympathetic neutrality and drive her into war. There would have been tremendous material advantages for Turkey in such a neutrality. Instead of being impoverished, bankrupt, utterly exhausted, wholly lost, as she now is, she might have been far richer than Roumania has ever been. There is one thing quite certain, and that is that Abdul-Hamid would never have let this golden opportunity slide of having a stream of money pouring in on himself and his country. And certainly Turkey would not have lacked moral justification had she so acted.

These considerations I have put forward rather from the Turkish anti-war point of view than from my own. They are opinions expressed hundreds of times by thoroughly patriotic and intelligent Turks who saw how the ever more intensive propaganda work of the German Ambassadors, first Marschall von Bieberstein, then Freiherr von Wangenheim, gradually wormed its way through opposition and prejudice, how the German Military Mission in Constantinople tried to turn the Russian hatred of Germany against

Turkey instead, how, finally, those optimists and jingoists on the "Committee," who knew as little about the true position of affairs throughout the world as they did of the intentions of the Entente or the means at their own disposal, proceeded to guide the ship of State more and more into German waters, without any reference to their own people, in return for promises won from Germany of personal power and material advantage. These were those days of excitement and smouldering unrest when Admiral von Souchon of the Goeben and the Breslau, with complete lack of discipline towards his superior, Djemal Pasha, arranged with the German Government to pull off a coup without Djemal's knowledge— chiefly because he was itching to possess the "Pour le Mérite" order— and sailed off with the Turkish Fleet to the Black Sea. (I have my information from the former American Ambassador in Constantinople, Mr. Morgenthau, who was furious at the whole affair.) [2]

These were the days when Enver and Talaat threw all their cards on the table in that fateful game of To Be or Not to Be, and brought on their country, scarcely yet recovered from the bloodshed of the Balkan War, a new and more terrible sacrifice of her manhood in a war extending over four, and later five, fronts. The whole result of this struggle for existence depended on final victory for Germany and that was becoming daily more doubtful; in fact, Ottoman troops had at last to be dispatched by German orders to the Balkans and Galicia.

Turkey had, too, to submit to the ignominy of making friends with her very recent enemy and preventing imminent military catastrophe by handing over the country along the Maritza, right up to the gates of the sacred city of Adrianople, to the Bulgarians. She had to look on while Armenia was conquered by the Russians;

---

[2] Djemal Pasha learnt the news that Admiral von Souchon had bombarded Russian ports, and so made war inevitable, one evening at the Club. Pale with rage, he sprang up and said: "So be it; but if things go wrong, Souchon will be the first to be hanged."

while Mesopotamia and Syria, in spite of initial successes, were threatened by English troops; while the "Holy War" came to an untimely end, the most consecrated of all Islam's holy places, Mecca, fell away from Turkey, the Arabs revolted and the Caliphate was shattered; while her population in the Interior endured the most terrible sufferings, and economic and financial life tended slowly and surely towards complete and hopeless collapse.

Not even yet, indeed now less than ever, is there any general acceptance among the people of the views held by Enver and Talaat and their acolytes. Not yet do intelligent, independent men believe the fine phrases of these minions of the "Committee," who are held in leading strings by these dictators partly through gifts of money, office, or the opportunity to enrich themselves at the expense of the people, partly through fear of the consequences should they revolt, or of those domestic servants who call themselves deputies and senators. On the contrary, it is no exaggeration to say that three-quarters of the intelligent out-and-out Turkish male population — quite apart from Levantines, Greeks, and Armenians — and practically the entire female population, who are more sensitive about the war and whose hearts are touched more deeply by its immeasurable suffering, have either remained perfectly friendly to England and France or have become so again through terrible want and suffering.

The consciousness that Turkey has committed an unbounded folly has long ago been borne in upon wide circles of Turks in spite of falsified reports and a stringent censorship. There would be no risk at all in taking on a wager that in private conversation with ten separate Turks, in no way connected with the "Committee," nine of them will admit, as soon as they know there is no chance of betrayal, that they do not believe Turkey will win, and that, with the exception of the much-feared Russia, they still feel as friendly as ever towards their present enemies. "Quoi qu'il arrive, c'est toujours la pauvre Turquie qui va payer le pot cassé." ("Whatever happens, it's always poor Turkey that'll have to pay the piper") and "Nous avons fait une grande gaffe" ("We have put our foot in it") were the kind of remarks made in every single political discussion I ever had in Constantinople —even with Turks.

So much for the men, who judge with their reason. What of the women? The one sigh of cultured Turkish women, up to the highest in the land—who should have a golden book written in their honour for their readiness to help, their sympathy, and humanity in this war—is: "When shall we get rid of the Boches; when will our good old friends, the English and the French, come back to us?" Nice results, these, of German propaganda, German culture, German brotherhood of arms! What a sad and shameful story for a German to have to tell! Naturally the drastic system of the military dictatorship precludes the public expression of such feelings, but one needs only have seen with one's own eyes the looks so often cast by even real Turkish cultured society at the German Feldgrauen who often marched in close formation through the streets of Constantinople—for a time they used to sing German soldiers' songs, until that was prohibited at the express wish of the Turkish Government to see how the land lies.

There was a marked and ill-concealed contrast in the coldness shown to Imperial German officers and the lavish affection showered on the Austrians and Hungarians who used for a time often to pass through Constantinople on their way to the Dardanelles or Anatolia with their heavy artillery. They were a great deal more sociable than their German comrades, and one could not fail to note the significance of such freely voiced comments as "N'est-ce pas, ils sont charmants les Autrichiens?" ("The Austrians are delightful, aren't they?") The sight of us Germans, especially the very considerable German garrison stationed for a time in the Capital, awakened in the Turks, however much they might recognise the military necessity for their presence, remarkable ideas about the future "German Egyptising of Turkey," and everyone blamed Enver Pasha as the man responsible for Germany's penetrating thus far.

A Turk in a high official position—whose name I shall naturally not divulge—even went so far as to say to me in an intimate personal discussion we were having one day between friend and friend: "We Turks are and will always remain, in spite of the war, pro-English and pro-French so far as social and intellectual life is concerned; and it would need twenty years of hard propaganda work on Germany's part, quite different from her present methods, to change this point of view, if it ever could be changed." He went on to recall the time of the pro-English era, and the enthusiastic demonstrations that had taken place at the Sirkedji station when the horses were taken out of the English Ambassador's carriage. "I was there myself," he said, "and believe me, apart from the war, heaps of us are at bottom still of the same mind." And, growing heated, he added: "What is your Embassy, tell me? Is it really an Embassy? No representation, no intimate intercourse with us, or at best only with your political agents, no personal charm, nothing but brusque demands and a most humiliating economic neglect of the Turkish population. The English and the French and even the Russians would treat us quite differently."

This man is no exception in his ideas. He is a thorough Young Turk, who holds with the "Committee" through thick and thin and has to thank them for a very pleasant billet, but he is, besides, a youngish man with a modern European education. He is thoroughly imbued, as are all of his kind, with modern French ideas, and even the war cannot alter that. It only needs the final collapse of the Central Powers, and then the break-down of the whole political system under the direction of these jingoistic emancipationists who think they can get on without Europe, and the Turks will all, every one of them, be as thoroughly pro-English and pro-French as they ever were and will hate Germany and everything German with fanatical hatred.

Towards Hungary, their blood relation, they will probably retain some friendliness in memory of their alliance in the Great War and the cause of Turanism; they will be quite indifferent to Bulgaria;

they will lose their fear of Russia and come to an agreement with her; but after the war there will be no bridging the gulf between Turkey and Germany, and if Germany, on the conclusion of peace, is allotted any part of smaller Turkey by the rest of the European Powers, she will have to reckon for many a long year with the very chilly relations that will exist between Germans and Turks. Even those who went heart and soul into the war as a war of defence against Turkey's powerful northern neighbour foresee that when peace is declared Turkey will, so far as her enormous indebtedness to Germany permits, rather throw herself on the mercy of England and France and America and beg from them the capital necessary for reconstruction and for freeing them from the hated German influence--an aversion which is already evident in hundreds of different ways. Even Germany is beginning to recognise the existence of this tendency, which, hand in hand with the jingoistic attempt to turkify commercial life, bodes ill for German activity in Turkey after the war.

These are the opinions of the educated classes. The people, however, the poor, ignorant Turkish people, were ready long ago to accept any solution that would liberate them from their terrible sufferings. The Turkish people have not the mental calibre of our German people which will perhaps make them fight on, just for the sake of leaving no stone unturned, even after it is quite evident that they are tending towards final collapse. The stake for which they are fighting is not so valuable to this agricultural people, who with an inferior and extortionate set of rulers have never been able really to enjoy life, as it is to the population of a modern industrial country like Germany, where every political gain or loss has a direct result on their own pockets; defeat will certainly have much less effect on the Oriental. One can therefore speak with confidence of a general longing for the end of the war at any price. The Turks have had quite enough of suffering, and there are limits to what even these willing and mutely resigned victims can bear.

Nevertheless it is quite certain that the courageous Turkish soldier, in obedience to iron discipline and in unconditional submission to his Padishah, will continue to defend his lost cause to the very last drop of his blood, with an unquestioning resignation that absolutely precludes the idea of any defection within the army. Only a purely political military revolution, originating with the better-informed officers, who now really no longer believe in ultimate victory, is within the bounds of possibility.

But the most confiding endurance on the part of the Turkish soldier, even when the military cause has long been lost, will not hinder this same soldier, when he is once more back in his own home as a peasant, from realising that European influence and European civilisation are a very competent protection against the miserably retrogressive Turkish rule, and that he has drawn more material profit from that single example of European activity, the Baghdad Railway, than from all Turkish official reforms put together, and so would willingly see Europe exercising a powerful control in his country. He would accept the military collapse of his country which he had so long and so bravely defended, and the dramatic political changes, with a quietly submissive "Inshallah." And although, deprived as he is of every kind of information and without even the beginnings of knowledge, he perhaps still believes in ultimate victory for the Padishah, he will probably heave a sigh of relief when the unexpected collapse comes, and he will not take long to understand what it means for him: freedom and happiness and an undreamt-of material well-being under strong European influence.

The late successor to the throne, Prince Yussuf Izzedin Effendi, was the highest of those in high authority who openly represented the pessimistic anti-war tendency. It was for this that he was murdered or perhaps made to commit suicide by Enver Pasha. The whole truth about this tragic occurrence can only be sifted to the bottom when the dictators of the "Committee" are no longer in their place and light finally breaks on Turkey. Whether it was murder or suicide, the death of the successor to the throne is one of the most dramatic scandals of Turkish history, and Enver Pasha has his blood, as well as the blood of so many others, on his head. As far as is possible during the war, Europe has already collected all the information available on the subject. I myself was in Constantinople when the tragic occurrence took place, and I can speak so far from personal experience.

In connection with this sensational event, the world has already heard how Yussuf Izzedin was kept for years under the despotic Abdul-Hamid shut off from the world as a semi-prisoner in his beautiful Konak of Sindjirli-kuyu, just outside the gates of Constantinople, where he became a sufferer from acute neurasthenia. In recent years, however, his health had improved and, although latently hostile to the men of the "Committee" and their politics, he had come more into the foreground, especially after the recapture of Adrianople, which he visited with full pomp and ceremony as Crown Prince of the Turkish Empire. While the Gallipoli campaign was going on, he even made a journey to the front to greet his soldiers. Early one morning he was found lying dead in a pool of his own blood with a severed artery. He had received his death wound in exactly the same place and exactly the same way as his father, Sultan Abdul-Aziz, who fell a victim to Abdul-Hamid's hatred. The political significance of Yussuf Izzedin's death is perfectly clear. What we want to do now is to demonstrate Enver Pasha's moral culpability in the matter and to show how he was more or less directly the murderer of this quiet, cultured, highly respected, and thoroughly patriotic man, who was some day to ascend the throne of Turkey.

So much at least seems to be clear, that Prince Izzedin, who was naturally interested in retaining his accession to the throne undisturbed and who in spite of his neurasthenia was man enough to stand up for his own rights, foresaw ruin for his kingdom by Turkey's entry into the war on the side of Germany. He was more far-seeing than the careless adventurers and narrow-minded fanatics of the "Committee" and recognised that the letting-go of the treasured Pan-Islamic traditions of old Sultan Hamid was a grave mistake which would lead to the alienation of the Arabs, and which endangered both the Ottoman Caliphate and Ottoman rule in the southern parts of the Empire. He could not console himself for the evacuation of the territory round Adrianople, right up to the gates of the sacred city, which meant much to him as the symbol of national enlightenment. He had a real personal dislike for upstarts of the stamp of Enver and Talaat. Apart from these differences of opinion and personal sympathies and antipathies, deep-rooted though these undoubtedly were, Yussuf Izzedin was and always would have been a thorough "Osmanli" with fiery nationalistic feelings, who wished for nothing but the good of his Empire and his country. And yet he was got rid of.

It would be difficult for the present Turkish Government to prove that the successor to the throne, apart from his feeling of sorrow that his country had been drawn into the war, apart from his readiness to conclude an honourable separate peace at the first possible moment, did anything which might have caused them trouble. The officials of the Turkish Government had themselves made repeated efforts through their Swiss Ambassadors to find out how the land lay, and whether they could conclude a separate peace; so they had no grounds at all for reproaching Prince Yussuf Izzedin, who, as a leader of this movement, naturally let no opportunity of this kind slide. But he was far too clever not to know that any attempt in this direction behind the backs of the present Government would have no chance of success so long as Turkey was held under the iron fist of Germany.

Perhaps the "Committee" had something to fear for the future, when the time came for the reverses now regarded as inevitable. Yussuf would then make use of his powerful influence in many circles—notably among the discontented retired military men—to demand redress from the "Committee." Enver, true to his unscrupulous character, quite hardened to the sight of Turkish blood, and determined to stick to his post at all costs—for it was not only lucrative, but flattering to his vanity—was not the man to stick at trifles with a poor neurasthenic, who under the present military dictatorship was absolutely at his mercy. He therefore decided on cold-blooded murder.

The Prince, well aware of the danger that threatened him, tried at the last moment to leave the country and flee to safety. He had even taken his ticket, and intended to start by the midday Balkan train next day to travel to Switzerland via Germany. He was forbidden to travel. Whether, feeling himself thus driven into a corner and nothing but death at the hand of Enver's creatures staring him in the face, he killed himself in desperation, or whether, as thousands of people in Constantinople firmly believe, and as would seem to be corroborated by the generally accepted, although of course not actually verified, tale of a bloody encounter between the murderers and the Prince's bodyguard, with victims on both sides, he was actually assassinated, is not yet settled, and it is really not a matter of vast importance.

One thing is clear, and that is that Izzedin Effendi did not pay with his life for any illoyal act, but merely for his personal and political opposition to Enver. He is but one on this murderer's long list of victims. The numerous doctors, all well known creatures of the "Committee" or easily won over by intimidation, who set their names as witnesses to this "suicide as a result of severe neurasthenia"— a most striking and suspicious similarity to the case of Abdul-Aziz—have not prevented one single thinking man in Constantinople from forming a correct opinion on the matter. The wily Turkish Government evidently chose this kind of death, just like his father's, so that they could diagnose the symptoms as those of incurable neurasthenia. History has already formed its own opinion as to how much freewill there was in Abdul-Aziz' death! The opinions of different people about Prince Yussuf's death only differ as to whether he was murdered or compelled to commit suicide. "On l'a suicidé" was the ironical and frank comment of one clever Old Turk. We will leave it at that.

The funeral of the successor to the throne was a most interesting sight. I sent an article on it to my paper at the time, which of course had only very, very slight allusions to anything of a sinister character; but it did not find favour with the censor at the Berlin Foreign Office. The editorial staff of the paper evidently saw what I was driving at, and wrote to me: "We have revised and touched up your report so as at least to save the most essential part of it;" but even the altered version did not pass the censor's blue pencil. But I had at any rate the moral satisfaction of knowing that of all the papers with correspondents in the Turkish capital, mine, the Kölnische Zeitung, was the only one that could publish nothing, not a single line, about this important and highly sensational occurrence, for I simply wrote nothing more. That was surely clear enough!

When in 1913, after the unsuccessful counter-revolution, Mahmud Shevket Pasha was assassinated and was going to be buried in Constantinople, the "Committee" issued invitations days beforehand to all foreign personages. This time nothing of the sort happened; and even the Press representatives were not invited to be present. On the former occasion everything possible was done, by putting off the interment as long as possible and repeatedly publishing the date, by lengthening the route of the funeral procession, to give several thousands of people an opportunity of taking part in the ceremony.

This time, however, the authorities arranged the burial with all speed, and the very next day after the sensational occurrence the body was hurried by the shortest way, through the Gülhané Park, to the Mausoleum of Sultan Mahmud-Moshee. The coffin had been quietly brought in the twilight the evening before from the Kiosk of Sindjirlikuyu on the other side of Pera on the Maslak Hill, to the top of the Serail. Along the whole route, however, wherever the public had access, there were lines of police and soldiers; and the bright uniforms of the police who were inserted in groups of twenty between every single row of the procession of Ministers, members of the "Committee" and delegaters who walked behind the coffin, were really the most conspicuous thing in the whole ceremony. Enver Pasha passed quite close to me, and neither I, nor my companions, could fail to note the ill-concealed expression of satisfaction on his face.

The most beautiful thing about this whole funeral, however, was the visit paid me by the Secretary-General of the Senate, the minute after I had reached home (and I had driven by the shortest way). With a zeal that might have surprised even the simplest minded of men, he offered to tell me about the Prince's life, lingering long and going into exhaustive detail over the well-known facts of his nervous ailment. Then, blushing at his own awkwardness and importunity, he begged me most earnestly to publish his version of all the details and circumstances of this tragic occurrence, "which no other paper will be in a position to publish." Naturally it was never written.

So, once more, in the late summer of 1916, Enver Pasha, who was so fond of discovering conspiracies and political movements in order to get rid of his enemies, and go scot free himself, had a fresh opportunity of reflecting, with even more foundation than usual, on the firmness of his position and the security of his own life.

It is perhaps time now to give a more comprehensive description of this man. We have already mentioned in connection with the failure of his Caucasus offensive that Enver has been extraordinarily overestimated in Europe. The famous Enver is neither a prominent intellectual leader nor a good organiser—in this direction he is far surpassed by Djemal Pasha —nor an important strategist. In military matters his positive qualities are personal courage, optimism, and, consequently, initiative which is never daunted by fear of consequences, also cold-bloodedness and determination; but he is entirely lacking in judgment, power of discrimination, and largeness of conception. From the German point of view he is particularly valuable for his unquestioning and unconditional association with the Central Powers, his readiness to do anything that will further their cause, his pliability and his zeal in accommodating himself even to the most trenchant reforms. But it is just these qualities that make enemies for him among retired military men and among the people.

Regarded from a purely personal point of view, Enver Pasha is, in spite of the fulsome praise showered on him by Germans inspired by that most pliant implement, German militarism, one of the most repugnant subjects ever produced by Turkey. Even from a purely external point of view his appearance does not at all correspond with the picture of him generally accepted in Germany from flattering reports and falsified photographs. Small of stature, with quite an ordinary face, he looks rather, as one of my journalistic colleagues said, like a "gardener's boy" than a Vice-General and War Minister, and anyone who ever has the opportunity I have so often had, of looking really closely at him, will certainly be repelled by his look of vanity and cunning. It was really most painful to have to listen to him (he has always been a bad and monotonous speaker) in the Senate and the Lower House at the conclusion of the Dardanelles campaign reading his report in a weak, halting voice, but with the disdainful tone of a dictator. Every third word was an "I." Even the Turkish Press accorded this parliamentary speech a fairly frosty reception.

Besides this, Enver is one of the most coldblooded liars imaginable. Time and again there has been no necessity for him to say certain things in Parliament, or to make certain promises, but apparently he found cynical enjoyment in making the people and Parliament feel their whole inferiority in his eyes. What can one think, for example, of such performances as this? At the end of 1916 when the discussion about military service for those who had paid the exemption tax (bedel) was going on, he gave an unsolicited and solemn assurance before the whole House that he had no intention whatever of calling up certain classes until the Bill had been finally passed and that it would show that he was really desirous of sparing commercial life as far as possible in the calling up of men. Exactly two hours after this speech the drum resounded through all the streets of Stamboul and Pera, calling up all those classes over which Enver had as yet no power of jurisdiction, and which he said he wanted to keep back because to tear them away from their employment would mean the complete disorganisation of the already sadly disordered commercial life of the country.

This was Talaat's opinion, too, and he offered a firm resistance to Enver's plan, which it appears had been introduced by command of the German Government. In this case, however, resistance was useless, and had to give way to military necessity. If Enver said something in Parliament—this at any rate was the general conclusion—one might be quite certain that exactly the opposite would take place. He has now gained for himself the reputation of being a liar and a murderer among all those who are not followers of the "Committee."

In contrast to Talaat, who is at least intelligent enough to keep up appearances and cunning enough to hold himself well in the background, Enver's personal lack of integrity in money matters is a subject of most shameful knowledge in Constantinople. It is pretty well generally known how he has made use of his position as Military Dictator to gain possession for himself of property worth thousands of pounds, and how in his financial dealings with Germany hundreds have found their way into his own pocket—up till the winter of 1915-1916, according to an estimate from confidential Turkish circles and from German sources I will not name, he had already managed to collect something like two million pounds, reckoned in English money. This son of a former lowly conducteur in the service of the Roads and Bridges Board, whose mother, as I have been assured by Turks is the case, plied in Stamboul the much-despised trade of "layer-out" of corpses, now lives in his Konak in more than princely luxury, with flowers and silver and gold on his table, having married, out of pure ambition, a very plain-looking princess. That is the true portrait of this much-coddled darling of the Young Turks, and latterly of the German people as well. This is the idol of so many admiring German women, who are bewitched by his more than adventurous career and the halo surrounding him which he has enhanced by every known and unknown means of self-advertisement. Enver's character won for him in "Committee" circles personal dislike and bitter, though veiled, enmity even from his colleagues who were of exactly the same political persuasion as himself. Of his relations towards the infinitely more important Djemal Pasha we have already spoken; we shall speak in a moment of his relations to Talaat. In the world of the retired military men, however, who had been badgered about by Enver, neglected and simply forcibly pensioned off by hundreds before the war because of their divergent political opinions, and even thrown into the street, the War Minister was heartily hated. A very large part of them were of the same political views as the murdered successor to the throne, and their opinion of the Great War was as we have already indicated. They pointed bitterly to Enver as the all-too-pliable servant of Germany, who was only too ready to sacrifice the flower of Ottoman youth on those far battlefields of Galicia at a sign from the German Staff, and open door after door to German influence in the Interior without even attempting to protect the land of his fathers from invasion and decay.

As we have said, political revolutions in Turkey usually start in military circles, not among the people, and there was an actual attempt in this direction in the autumn of 1916. Either by chance or by someone's betraying the plot, it was discovered by Enver in time, and the number of military men and Old Turkish personages associated with them, imprisoned in Constantinople alone, reached six hundred. At the head of the movement stood Major Yakub Djemil Bey.

During the whole of the summer of 1916 Enver's position had been looked upon as quite insecure. The knowledge of his greed in money matters, his tactless pushing, and his ruthless brutality had totally alienated a wide circle of people, and many believed that he would soon have to resign.

In addition to this, a deep inward antagonism reigned between him and Talaat, the real leader and by far the most important statesman of Turkey, which was far more than a cleverly veiled personal dislike. There was a constant struggle for power going on between the two men. By the end of May the crisis had become pretty acute, although outward appearances were still preserved and only well-informed circles knew anything at all about the matter. Enver had at that time to hurry back from the Irak, where he was on a visit of inspection with the German Chief of Staff and the Military Attaché, in order to safeguard his post. In confidential circles, the outbreak of open enmity between the two was fully expected; but this time again Talaat was the cleverer. He felt that, in spite of his own greater influence and following, in spite of his real superiority to Enver, he might perhaps, if he tried conclusions with him while he was still in command of the army, find himself the loser and, in view of Enver's murderous habits, pay for his rashness with his life. So he decided not to risk a decisive battle just yet. He was too patriotic, also, to let things come to an open break during the difficult time of war. Talaat disappeared for a short time on a visit of inspection to Angora, and things settled down to their old way again.

There is still internal conflict going on. But Enver, with boundless ambition and no fine feelings of honour, clings to his post, and has shown by the way he dealt with the instigators of the conspiracy mentioned above that nothing but force will move him from his post, and that he will never yield to public opinion or the criticism of his colleagues. He was troubled by no qualms, in spite of the widely circulated opinion that he would certainly jeopardise his life if he went on in the same ruthless way towards the retired military men. He simply had the leader, Yakub Djemil Bey, hanged like a common criminal, and the whole of his followers, for the most part superior officers and highly respected persons, turned into soldiers of the second class, and put in the front-line trenches.

Enver's removal would not alter the whole Young Turkish regime much, but it would take from it much of its ruthless barbarity, and its most repugnant representative would vanish from the picture. It would also be a severe blow for Germany and her militaristic policy of driving Turkey mercilessly to suicide. It would be a godsend to the anti-German Djemal Pasha. From a political point of view it would mean, far more than Talaat's appointment as Grand Vizier, the absolute supremacy of that statesman.

At bottom probably less ruthless than Enver and certainly cleverer, there is no doubt but that he would pursue his jingoistic ideas in the realm of race-politics, but at any rate he would not want any military system of frightfulness. Enver's removal from office will come within the range of near possibility as soon as the new British operations against Southern Palestine and Mesopotamia have produced a real victory. Turkey is not in a good enough military position to prevent this, and the whole world will soon recognise that it is this servant of Germany, this careless optimist and very mediocre strategist who is to blame for the inexorable breaking-up of the Ottoman Empire.

The contrast I have noted between Enver and Talaat provides the opportunity for saying a few words about Talaat, now Pasha and Grand Vizier, and by far the most important man of New Turkey. As Minister of the Interior, he has guided the whole fate of his country, except in purely military matters, as uncrowned king. It is he more than anyone else who is the originator of the whole system of home politics. Solidity of character, earnestness, freedom from careless optimism, and conspicuous power of judgment distinguish him most favourably from Enver, who possesses the opposite of all these qualities. A high degree of intelligence, an enormous knowledge of men, an exceptional gift of organisation and tireless energy combined with great personal authority, prudence and reserve, calm weighing of the actual possibilities—in a word, all the qualities of the real statesman—raise him head and shoulders above the whole of his colleagues and co-workers. It would be unjust to doubt his ardent patriotism or the honesty of his ideas and intentions. Talaat's character is so impressive that one often hears even Armenians, the victims of his own original policy of persecution, speak of him with respect, and I have even heard the opinion expressed that had it not been for Talaat's cleverness, the Committee would have gone much further with their mischievous policy.

But his high intellectual abilities do not prevent him from suffering from that same plague of narrow-minded, jingoistic illusion peculiar to the Pan-Turks. He is as if intoxicated with a race-fanaticism that stifles all nobler emotions. Talaat is too methodical and clever not to avoid all intentional ruthlessness, but in practice his system, which he follows out with inflexible logic to the bitter end, turns out to be just as brutal as Enver's intrinsically more brutal policy. And although he accommodates himself outwardly to modern European methods and knows how to utilise them, the ethics of his system are out-and-out Asiatic. When Talaat speaks in the "Committee," there is very rarely the slightest opposition. He has usually prepared and coached the "Committee" so well beforehand that he can to all appearance keep in the background and only follow the majority. With the exception of a few military affairs, everything has always taken place that he has proposed in Parliament.

Beside this man, whose sparkling eyes, massive shoulders, broad chest, clean-cut profile and exuberant health denote the whole unbounded energy of the dictator, the good-natured, degenerate, and epileptically inclined Sultan, Mehmed V, "El Ghazi" ("the hero"), is but a weak shadow. But if we fully recognise Talaat's high intellectual qualities, we should like all the more to emphasise that he must be held personally responsible more than all the others for everything that is now happening in Turkey, so far as it is not of a military character. The spirit reigning in Turkey to-day, the spirit of Pan-Turkish jingoism, is Talaat's spirit. The Armenian persecutions are his very own work. And when the day of reckoning comes for the Turkey of the "Committee of Union and Progress," it is to be hoped that Europe as judge and chastiser and avenger of an outraged civilisation, will lay the chief blame on Talaat Pasha rather than on his far weaker colleague Enver.

All his eminent qualities, however, do not prevent this intellectual leader of Turkey, the most important man, beside the Sultan, in the land, from showing signs of something that is typical of the whole "Committee" clique with their dictatorial power, and which we may perhaps be allowed to call parvenuishness. At all points we see the characteristics of the parvenu in this statesman and one-time adventurer and in these creatures of the "Committee" who have recently become wealthy by certain abuses—I would remind you only of the Requisitions— and by a lucrative adherence to the ruling clique. There are of course individual cases of distinguished men of good birth throwing in their lot with the "Committee," but they are extremely rare, and they only help to give an even worse impression of the average Young Turk belonging to the Government. Their past is usually extremely doubtful, and their careers have been somewhat varied.

No one of course would ever think of setting it down as a black mark against Talaat, for example, that he had to work his way up to his present supreme position from the very modest occupation of postman and postal coach conductor on the Adrianople road, via telegraph assistant and other branches of the Post Office; on the contrary, such intelligence and energy are worthy of the highest praise. But Talaat's case is a comparatively good one, and it is not so much their low social origin that is a drawback to these political leaders of Turkey, as their complete lack of education in statesmanship and history, which unfits them for the high rôle they are called upon to fill. Naturally it is not exactly pleasant when a man like Herr Paul Weitz, the correspondent of the Frankfurter

Zeitung, and a political agent, can boast with a certain amount of justification that he has given tips of money to many of the present members of the "Committee"—in the real sense of the word, not in the political meaning of backshish! It is no wonder, then, that German influence won its way through so easily!

Even yet Talaat's lowly origin is a drawback to him socially, and, in spite of his jovial manner and his complete confidence in his own powers, he sometimes feels himself so unsure that he rather avoids social duties. Probably one of the reasons of his long delay in accepting the post of Grand Vizier—he was already definitely marked out for it in the summer of 1915—was his own inner consciousness that his whole past life unfitted him socially for the duties of such an office. That he has now decided to accept it, is only the logical sequence of the system of absolute Turkification, which, with its plan of muzzling and supplanting all non-Turkish elements, had of course to get rid of the Egyptian element in the Government, represented by Prince Halim Saïd, the late Grand Vizier, and his brother, the late Minister of Public Works.

There are far more outstanding cases of incompatibility between social upbringing and present activity among the "Committee." I will simply take the single example of the Director General of the Press, Hikmet Bey. Mischievous Pera still gives him the nickname of "Sütdji" ("milkman"), because—although it is no reproach to him any more than in Talaat's case—he still kept his father's milk shop in the Rue Tepé Bashi in Pera before he managed to get himself launched on a political career by close adherence to the Committee. Sometimes, of course, one inherits from a low social origin far worse things than social inferiority. Perhaps Djemal Pasha's murderous instincts are to be traced to the fact that his grandfather was the official hangman in the service of Sultan Mahmud, and that his father still retained the nick-name of "hangman" among the people.

One only needs to cast a glance at the Young Turks who are the

132

leaders of fashion in the "Club de Constantinople"—after the English and French members are absent—with German officers who have been admitted as temporary members at a reduced subscription, and one will find there, as in the more exclusive "Cercle d'Orient," and in the "Yachting Club" in Prinkipo in the summer-time, individuals belonging to the "Committee" whose lowly origin and bad manners are evident at the first glance. Talaat, who is himself President of the Club, knows exactly how to get his adherents elected as members without one of them being blackballed. People who used not to know what an International Club was, and who perhaps, in accordance with their former social status, got as far as the vestibule to speak to the Concierge, are now great "club men" and can afford, with the money they have amassed in "clique" trade and by the famous system of Requisitions, to play poker every evening for stakes of hundreds of Turkish pounds. One single kaleidoscopic glance into the perpetual whirl of any one of these clubs, which used to be places of friendly social intercourse for the best European circles, is quite sufficient to see the class of degenerate, greedy parvenus that rule poor, bleeding, helpless, exhausted Turkey. One cannot but be filled with a deep sympathy for this unfortunate land.

The Turks of decent birth are disgusted at these parvenus, I have had conversations with many an old Pasha and Senator, true representatives of the refined and kindly Old Turkish aristocracy, and heard many a word of stern disapproval of the "Committee" quite apart from their divergent political opinions. There is a whole distinguished Turkish world in Constantinople who completely "boycott Enver and his consorts socially, although they have to put up with their caprices politically. "I don't know Enver at all," or "Je ne connais pas ces gens-là" ("I don't know these people"), are phrases that one very often hears repeated with infinite disdain. In all these cases it is the purely personal side—birth and manners—that repels them.

Socially the cleft between the two camps is far deeper than it is politically, for many of these same people accommodate themselves, though with reluctance in their heart, to sharing at least formally as Senators in the responsibility for the present Young Turkish policy. They have to do so, for otherwise they would simply be flung mercilessly by Enver's Clique on to the streets to beg for bread. This is how it comes about to-day that, with very few exceptions, the Senators, who, to tell the truth, have as little practical say as the members of the Lower House, are all outwardly complaisant followers of the "Committee." The more doctrinal, but at any rate courageous and honourable opposition of Ahmed Riza is likewise of very little significance. Once, about the middle of December, 1916, Enver even went so far as to hurl the epithet "shameless dog" at Ahmed Riza in the Senate without being called to order by the President.

The Deputies are also, with even fewer exceptions than the Senators—only one or two are reasonable men—all slaves pure and simple of Enver and Talaat. The Lower House is nothing but a set of employees paid by the Clique. In other countries now at war the Lower House may have sunk to the level of a laughing-stock; in Turkey it has become the instrument of crime. And it is these same toadies and parasites, who daily carry out this military dictator's will in Parliament, that he daily treats with scarcely veiled irony and open and complete disdain. These are the "representatives of the people" in Turkey in wartime!

CHAPTER X

The outlook for the future—The consequences of trusting Germany—The Entente's death sentence on Turkey—The social necessity for this deliverance— Anatolia, the new Turkey after the war—Forecasts about the Turkish race—The Turkish element in the lost territory—Russia and Constantinople; international guarantees—Germany, at peace, benefits too—Farewell to the German "World-politicians" —German interests in a victorious and in an amputated Turkey—The German-Turkish treaty—A paradise on earth—The Russian commercial impetus —The new Armenia—Western Anatolia, the old Greek centre of civilisation—Great Arabia and Syria—The reconciliation of Germany.

We have come to the end of our sketches. The question before us now is: What will become of Turkey ? The Entente has pronounced formal sentence of death on the Empire of the Sultan, and neither the slowly fading military power of Turkey, nor the help of Germany, who is herself already virtually conquered, will be able to arrest her fate.

On the high frost-bound uplands of Armenia the Russians hold a strategic position from which it is impossible to dislodge them, and which will probably very soon extend to the Gulf of Alexandretta. In Mesopotamia, after that enormously important political event, the Fall of Baghdad, the union was effected between the British troops and the Russians, advancing steadily from Persia. The Suez Canal is now no longer threatened, and the British troops have been removed from there for a counter-offensive in Southern Palestine, and probably, when the psychological moment arrives, an offensive against Syria, now so sadly shattered politically. It is quite within the bounds of possibility, too, that during this war a big new Front may be formed in Western Anatolia, already completely broken up by the Pan-Hellenic Irredenta, and the Turks will be hard put to it to find troops to meet the new offensive. Arabia is finally and absolutely lost, and England, by establishing an Arabian Caliphate, has already won the war against Turkey. Meantime, on the far battlefields of Galicia and the Balkans, whole Ottoman divisions are pouring out their lifeblood, fighting for that elusive German victory that never comes any nearer, while in every nook and corner of their own land there is a terrible lack of troops. Enver Pasha, at length grown anxious, has attempted to recall them, but in vain.

That is a short résumé of the military situation. This is how the Turkey of Enver and Talaat is atoning for the trust she has placed in Germany.

To a German journalist who went out two years ago to a great Turkey, striving for a "Greater Turkey," it does indeed seem a bitter irony of fate to see his sphere of labour thus reduced to nothingness. The fall of Turkey is the greatest blow that could have been dealt to German "world-politics"; it is a disappointment that will have the gravest consequences. But from the standpoint of culture, human civilisation, ethics, the liberty of the peoples and justice, historical progress, the economic development of wide tracts of land of the greatest importance from their geographical position, it is one of the most brilliant results of the war, and one to be hailed with unmixed joy. When I look back on how wonderfully things have shaped in the last two and a half years I am bound to admit that I am happy things have turned out as they have. If perchance any Turk who knows me happens to read these lines, I beg him not to think that my ideas are saturated with hatred of Turkey. On the contrary, I love the country and the Turkish race with those many attractive qualities that rightly appealed to a poet like Loti.

I have asked myself thousands of times what would be the best political solution of the problem, how to help this people—and the other races inhabiting their country—to true and lasting happiness. From my many journeys in tropical lands, I have grown accustomed to the sight of autochthonous civilisations and semi-civilised peoples, and am as interested in them as in the most perfectly civilised nations of Europe. I have therefore, I think, been able to set aside entirely in my own mind the territorial interests of the West in the development of the Near East, and give my whole attention to Turkey's own good and Turkey's own needs. But even then I have been obliged to subscribe to the sentence of death passed on the Turkey of the Young Turks and the sovereignty of the Ottoman Empire. It is with the fullest consciousness of what I am doing that I agree to the only seemingly cruel amputation of this State. It is merely the outer shell covering a number of peoples who suffer cruelly under an unjust system, chief among them the brave Turkish people who have been led by a criminal Government to take the last step on the road to ruin. The point of view I have adopted does not in any way detract from my personal sympathies, and I still have hopes that the many personal friendships I made in Constantinople will not be broken by the hard words I have been obliged to utter in the cause of truth, in the interests of outraged civilisation, and in the interests of a happier future for the Ottoman people themselves.

The amputation of Turkey is a stern social necessity. Someone has said: "The greatest enemy of Turkey is the Turk." I have too much love for the Turkish people, too much sympathy for them, to adopt this pessimistic attitude without great inward opposition; but unfortunately it is only too true. We have seen how the Turkey of Enver and Talaat has reacted sharply against the Western-minded, liberal era of the 1876 and 1908 constitutions, and has turned again to Asia and her newly discovered ideal, Turanism. To the Turks of to-day, European culture and civilisation are at best but a technical means; they are no longer an end in themselves. Their dream is no longer Western Europe, but a nationally awakened and strengthened Asiatentum.

In face of this intellectual development, how can we hope that in the new Turkey there will be a radical alteration of what, in the whole course of Ottoman history, has always been the one characteristic, unchangeable, momentous fact, of what has always shattered the most honest efforts at reform, and always will shatter every attempt at improvement within a sovereign Turkey—I refer to the relationship of the Turk to the "Rajah" (the "herd"), the Christian subjects of the Padishah. The Ottoman, the Mohammedan conqueror, lives by the "herd" he has found in the land he has conquered; the "herd" are the "unbelievers," and rooted deep in the mind of this sovereign people, who have never quite lost their nomadic instincts, is the conviction that they have the right to live by the sweat of the brow of their Christian subjects and on the fruits of their labour. That we Europeans think this unjust the Turk will never be able to grasp.

A Wali of Erzerum once said: "The Turkish Government and the Armenian people stand in the relationship of man and wife, and any third persons who feel sympathy for the wife and anger at the wife-beating husband will do better not to meddle in this domestic strife." This quotation has become famous, for it exactly characterises the relationship of the Turk to the "Rajah," not to the Armenians. In this phrase alone there lies, quite apart from all the crimes committed by the present Turkish Government, a sufficient moral and political foundation for the sentence of death passed on the sovereignty of the present Turkish State. For so long as the Turks cling to Islam, from which springs that opposition between Moslem rulers and "Giaur" subjects so detrimental to all social progress, it is Europe's sacred duty not to give Turkey sovereignty over any territory with a strong Christian element. That is why Turkey must at all costs be confined to Inner Anatolia; that is why complete amputation is necessary; and why the outlying districts of Turkey, the Straits, the Anatolian coast, the whole of Armenia must be rescued and, part of it at any rate, placed under formal European protection.

Even in Inner Anatolia, which will probably still be left to the Ottomans after the war, the strongest European influence must be brought to bear—which will probably not be difficult in view of

Turkey's financial bankruptcy; European customs and civilisation must be introduced; in a word, Europe must exercise sufficient control to be in a position to prevent the numerous non-Turks resident even in Anatolia from being exposed to the old system of exploiting the "Rajah." Discerning Turks themselves have admitted that it would be best for Europe to put the whole of Turkey for a generation under curatorship and general European supervision.

I, personally, should not be satisfied with this system for the districts occupied more by non-Turks than by Turks; but, on the other hand, I should not go so far in the case of Inner Anatolia. I trust that strong European influence will make it possible to make Inner Anatolia a sovereign territory. I have pinned my faith on the Ottoman race being given another and final opportunity on her own ground of showing how she will develop now after the wonderful intellectual improvement that has taken place during the war. I hope at the same time that even in a sovereign Turkish Inner Anatolia Europe will have enough say to prevent any out-growths of the "Rajah principle."

The Turks must not be deprived of the opportunity to bring their new-found abilities, which even we must praise, to bear on the production of a new, modern, but thoroughly Turkish civilisation of their own on their own ground. Anatolia, beautiful and capable of development, is, even if we confine it to those interior parts chiefly inhabited by Ottomans, still quite a big enough field for the production of such a civilisation; it is quite big enough too for the terribly reduced numbers now belonging to the Osmanic race.

The amputation and limitation of Turkey, even if they do not succeed in altering the real Turkish point of view—and this, so far as the relationship to the Christians is concerned, is the same, from the Pasha down to the poorest Anatolian peasant—will at least have a tremendously beneficial effect. The possibilities in the Turkish race will come to flower. "The worst patriots," I once dared to say in one of my articles in spite of the censorship, "are not those who look for the future of the nation in concentrated cultural work in the Turkish nucleus-land of Anatolia, instead of gaping over the Caucasus and down into the sands of the African desert in their search for a 'Greater Turkey.' " And in connection with the series of lectures I have already mentioned about Anatolian hygiene and social politics, I said, with quite unmistakable meaning: "Turkey will have a wonderful opportunity on her own original ground, in the nucleus-land of the Ottomans, of proving her capability and showing that she has become a really modern, civilised State."

My earnest wish is that all the Turks' high intellectual abilities, brought to the front by this war, may be concentrated on this beautiful and repaying task. Intensive labour and the concentration of all forces on positive work in the direction of civilisation will have to take the place of corrupt rule, boundless neglect, waste, the strangulation of all progressive movements, political illusions, the unquenchable desire for conquest and oppression. This is what we pray for for Anatolia, the real New Turkey after the war. In other districts, also, now fully under European control, the pure Turkish element will flourish much more exceedingly than ever before under the beneficent protection of modern, civilised Governments. Frankly, the dream of Turkish Power has vanished. But new life springs out of ruin and decay; the history of mankind is a continual change.

Russia, too, after war, will no longer be what she seemed to terrified Turkish eyes and jealous German eyes dazzled by "world-politics": a colossal creature, stretching forth enormous suckers to swallow up her smaller neighbours; a country ruled by a dull, unthinking despotism.

From the standpoint of universal civilisation it is to be hoped that the solution of the problem of the Near East will be to transform the Straits between the Black Sea and Aegea, together with the city of Constantinople, uniquely situated as it is, into a completely international stretch with open harbours. Then we need no longer oppose Russian aspirations. If England, the stronghold of Free Trade and of all principles of freedom of intercourse, and France, the land of culture, interested in Turkey to the extent of millions, were content to leave Russia a free hand in the Straits; if Roumania, shut in in the Black Sea, did not fear for her trade, but was willing to become an ally of Russia in full knowledge of the Entente agreement about the Straits, it is of course sufficiently evident what guarantee with regard to international freedom modern Russia will have to give after the war, and even the Germans have nothing to fear. Of course the German anti-European "Antwerp-Baghdad" dream will be shattered. But once Germany is at peace, she will probably find that even the Russian solution of the Straits question benefits her not a little. The final realisation of Russia's efforts, justifiable both historically and geographically, to reach the Mediterranean at this one eminently suitable spot, will certainly contribute in an extraordinary degree to remove the unbearable political pressure from Europe and ensure peace for the world.

Just a few parting words to the German "World-politicians." Very often, as I have said, I heard during my stay in Constantinople expressions of anxiety on the part of Germans that all German interests, even purely commercial ones, would be gravely endangered in the victorious New Turkey, which would spring to life again with renewed jingoistic passions and renewed efforts at emancipation. And more than once—all honour to the feelings of justice and the sound common sense of those who dared to utter such opinions—I was told by Germans, in the middle of the war, and with no attempt at concealment, that they fully agreed it was an absolute necessity for Russia to have the control of the only outlet for her enormous trade to the Mediterranean, and that commercially at any rate the fight for Constantinople and the Straits was a fight for a just cause.

Now, let us take these two points of view together. From the purely German standpoint, which is better?—a victorious and self-governing Turkey imbued with jingoism and the desire for emancipation, practically closed to us, even commercially, or an amputated Turkey, compelled to appeal for European help and European capital to recover from her state of complete exhaustion; a Turkey freed from those Young Turkish jingoists who, in spite of all their fine phrases and the German help they had to accept for all their inward distaste of it, hate us from the very depths of their heart; a Turkey which, even if Russia, —as a last resort!—is allowed to become mistress of the Dardanelles with huge international guarantees, would, in the Anatolia that is left to her, capable of development as it is, and rich in national wealth, offer a very considerable field of activity for German enterprise? The short-sighted Pan-Germans, who are now fighting for the victory of anti-foreign neo-Pan-Turkism against the modern, civilised States of the Entente, who had no wish at all that Germany should not fare as well as the rest in the wide domains of Asiatic Turkey, can perhaps answer my question. They should have asked themselves this, and foreseen the consequences before they yielded weakly to Turkish caprices and themselves stirred up the Turks against Europe.

As things stand now, however, the German Government has thought fit, in her blind belief in ultimate victory, to enter on a formal treaty, guaranteeing the territorial integrity of the Ottoman Empire, at a point in the war when no reasonable being even in Germany could possibly still believe that a German victory would suffice to protect Turkey after she has been solemnly condemned by the Entente for her long list of crimes. Germany has thus given a negative answer to the question passed from mouth to mouth in the international district of Pera almost right from Turkey's entry into the war: "Will Germany, if necessary, sacrifice Constantinople and the Dardanelles, if she can thus secure peace with Russia?" She had already given the answer "No" before the absurd illusions of a possible separate peace with Russia at this price were finally and utterly dispelled by the speech of the Russian Minister Trepoff, and the purposeful and cruelly clear refusal of Germany's offer of peace. These events and the increasing excitement about the war in

Constantinople and elsewhere were not required to show that in the Near East as well the fight must be fought "to the bitter end."

Never, however—and that is German World-politics, and the ethics of the World-politician—have I ever heard a single one of those Germans, who thought it an impossibility to sacrifice their ally Turkey in order to gain the desired peace, put forward as an argument for his opinion the shame of a broken promise, but only the consideration that German activity in the lands of Islam, and particularly in the valuable Near East, would be over and done with for ever. I wonder if those who have decided, with the phantom of a German-Turkish victory ever before them, to go on with the struggle on the side of Turkey even after she had committed such abominable crimes, and to drench Europe still further with the blood of all the civilised nations of the world, ever have any qualms as to how much of their once brilliant possibilities of commercial activity in Turkey, now so lightly staked, would still exist were Turkey victorious.

Luckily for mankind, history has decided otherwise. After the war, the huge and flourishing trade of Southern Russia will be carried down to the then open seaports between Europe and Asia; the wealth of Odessa and the Pontus ports, enormously increased and free to develop, will be concentrated on the Bosporus and the Dardanelles, and the whole hitherto neglected city of Constantinople, from Pera and Galata to Stamboul and Scutari and Haidar-Pasha, will become an earthly paradise of pulsing life, well-being, and comfort. The luxury and elegance of the Crimea will move southwards to these shores of unique natural beauty and mild climate which form the bridge between two continents and between two seas. Anyone who returns after a decade of peaceful labour, when the Old World has recovered from its wounds, to the Bosporus and the shores of the Sea of Marmora, which he knew before the war, under Turkish regime, will be astonished at the marvellous changes which will then have been wrought in that favoured corner of the earth.

Never, even after another hundred years of Turkish rule, would that unique coast ever have become what it can be and what it must be—one of the very greatest centres of international intercourse and the Riviera of the East, not only in beauty of landscape, but in luxury and wealth. The greatest stress in this connection is to be laid on the lively Russian impetus that will spring from a modernised Russia, untrammelled by restrictions in the Straits. Convinced as I am that Russia after the war will no longer be the Russia of to-day, so feared by Germany, the Balkan States, and Turkey, I am prepared to give this impetus full play, as being the best possible means for the further development of Constantinople.

In Asia Minor, from Brussa to the slopes of the Taurus and the foot of the Armenian mountains, there will extend a modern Turkey which has finally come to rest, to concentration, to peaceful labour, after centuries of conflict, despotic extortion, the suicidal policy of military adventurers, and superficial attempts at expansion coupled with neglect of the most important internal duties. The inhabitants of these lands will soon have forgotten that "Greater Turkey" has collapsed. They will be really happy at last, these people whose idea of happiness hitherto had been a veneer of material well-being obtained by toadying, while the great bulk of the Empire pined in dirt, ignorance, and poverty, consumed by an outworn militarism, oppressed by a decaying administration. Then, but not till then, the world will see what the Turkish people is capable of. Then there will be no need for pessimism about this kindly and honourable race. Then we can become honest "Pro-Turks" again.

In Western Asia Minor, Europe will not forget that the whole shore, where once stood Troy, Ephesus, and Milet, is an out-and-out Hellenic centre of civilisation. Quite independently of all political feelings towards present-day Greece, this historical fact must be taken into consideration in the final ruling. It is to be hoped that the Greek people will not have to atone for ever for the faults of their non-Greek king who has forgotten that it is his sacred duty to be a

144

Greek and nothing but a Greek, and who has betrayed the honour and the future of the nation.

The Armenian mountain-land, laid waste by war, and emptied of men by Talaat's passion for persecution, will obtain autonomy from her conqueror, Russia, and will perhaps be linked up with all the other parts of the east, inhabited by the last remnants of the Armenian people. Armenia, with its central position and divided into three among Turkey, Russia, and Persia, may from its geographical position, its unfortunate history, and the endless sufferings it has been called upon to bear, be called the Poland of Further Asia. Delivered from the Turkish system, freed from all antagonistic Turko-Russian military principles of obstruction, linked up by railways to the west as well as the already well-developed region of Transcaucasia, with a big through trade from the Black Sea via Trapezunt to Persia and Mesopotamia, it will once more offer an excellent field of activity to the high intellectual and commercial abilities of its people, now, alas! scattered to the four winds of heaven. But they will return to their old home, bringing with them European ideas, European technique, and the most modern methods from America.

If men are lacking, they can be obtained from the near Caucasus with its narrow, overfilled valleys, inhabited by a most superior race of men, who have always had strong emigrating instincts. Even this most unfortunate country in the whole world, which the Turks of the Old Regime and of the New have systematically mutilated and at last bequeathed to Russia with practically not a man left, is going to have its spring-time.

In the south, Great Arabia and Syria will have autonomy under the protection of England and France with their skilful Islam policy ; they will have the benefit of the approved methods of progressive work in Egypt, the Soudan, and India as well as the Atlas lands; they will be exposed to the influences and incitements of the rest of civilised Europe; they will probably be enriched with capital from

145

America, where thousands of Arab and Syrian, as well as Armenian, refugees have found a home; they will provide the first opportunity in history of showing how the Arab race accommodates itself to modern civilisation on its own ground and with its own sovereign administration. The final deliverance of the Arabs from the oppressive and harmful supremacy of the Turks, now happily accomplished by the war, was one of the most urgent demands for a race that can look back on centuries of brilliant civilisation. The civilised world will watch with the keenest interest the self-development of the Arabian lands.

Even Germany, once she is at peace, will have no need to grumble at these arrangements, however diametrically opposed they may be to the now sadly shattered plans of the Pan-German and Expansion politicians. Germany will not lose the countless millions she has invested in Turkey. She will have her full and sufficient share in the European work and commercial activity that will soon revive again in the Near East. The Baghdad railway of "Rohrbach & Company" will never be built, it is true; but the Baghdad Railway with a loyal international marking off of the different zones of interest, the Baghdad Railway, as a huge artery of peaceful intercourse linking up the whole of Asia Minor and bringing peace and commercial prosperity, will all the more surely rise from its ruins. And when once the German Weltpolitik with its jealousy, its tactless, sword-rattling interference in the time-honoured vital interests of other States, its political intrigues disguised in commercial dress, is safely dead and buried, there will be nothing whatever to hinder Germany from making use of this railway and carrying her purely commercial energy and the products of her peaceful labour to the shores of the Persian Gulf and receiving in return the rich fruits of her cultural activity on the soil of Asia Minor.

APPENDIX

For the better understanding of the fact that a German journalist, the representative of a great national paper like the Kölnische Zeitung, could publish such a book as this, and to ward off in advance all the furious personal attacks which will result from its publication, and which might, without an explanation, injuriously affect its value as an independent and uninfluenced document, it is, I think, essential to explain the rôle I filled in Constantinople, how I left Turkey, and how I came to the decision to publish my experiences.

As far as my post on the Kölnische Zeitung is concerned, I accepted it and went to Turkey although I was from the very beginning against German "World-politics" of the present-day style at any rate (not against German commercial and cultural activity in foreign countries) and against militarism—as was only to be expected from one who had studied colonial politics and universal history unreservedly, and had spent many years studying in the English, French, and German colonies of Africa—and although I was quite convinced that Germany's was the crime of setting the war in motion. Besides, my "anti-militarism" is not of a dogmatic kind, but refers merely to the relations customary between civilised nations— witness the fact that I took part in the Colonial War of 1904-6 in German South-West Africa as a volunteer.

I hoped to find in Turkey some satisfaction for my extra-European leanings, a sphere of labour less absorbed by German militarism, and opportunity for independent study, and surely no one will take it amiss that I seized such a chance, certainly unique in war-time, in spite of my political views.

Once arrived in Turkey, I kept well in the background to begin with, so as to be able to form my own opinion, of course doing my uttermost at the same time to be loyal to the task I had undertaken. In spite of everything I had to witness, it was quite easy to reconcile all oppositions, until that famous day when my wife denounced Germany to my face. From that moment I became an enemy of present-day Germany and began to think of one day publishing the whole truth about the system. Until then I had contented myself with never saying a good word about the war, as one can easily find for oneself from a perusal of my various articles in the Kölnische Zeitung during 1915-16, dated from Constantinople and marked (a small steamship).

That dramatic event which finally alienated me from the German cause took place just after the end of a severe crisis in my relationship with German-Turkish Headquarters. Some slight hints I had given of Turkish mismanagement, cynicism, and jingoism in a series of articles appearing from February 15th, 1916, onwards, under the title "Turkish Economic Problems," so far as they were possible under existing censorship conditions, was the occasion of the trouble. One can imagine that Headquarters would certainly be furious with a journalist whose articles appeared one fine day, literally translated, in the Matin under the title: "Situation insupportable en Turquie, décrite par un journaliste allemand" ("Insufferable situation in Turkey, described by a German journalist"), and cropped up once more on June 1st, in the Journal des Balcans. I was three times over threatened with dismissal. My paper sent a confidential man to hold an inquiry, and after a month he made a confidential report, which resulted in my being allowed to remain. But the fact that the same journalist that wrote such things was married to a Czech was too much for my colleagues, who were in part in the pay of the Embassy, in part in the pay of the Young Turkish Committee, whose politics they praised; regardless of their own inward convictions, like the representative of the Berliner Tageblatt, to get material benefit or make sure of their own jobs. I gleaned many humorous details at a nightly sitting of my Press colleagues in Pera, at which I myself was branded as a "dangerous character that must be got rid of," and my wife (who

was far too young ever to worry about politics) as a "Russian spy"—
perhaps because, with the justifiable pride and reserve of her race,
she did not attempt to cultivate the society of the German colony.
That began the period of intrigues and ill-will, but my enemies did
not succeed in damaging me, although matters went so far as a
denunciation of me before the "Prevention of Espionage
Department" of the General Staff in Berlin. My paper, after they had
given me the fullest moral satisfaction, and had arranged for me to
remain in Constantinople in spite of all that had taken place,
thought it was better to give me the chance of changing and offered
me a new post on the editorial staff elsewhere.

However, I was now quite finished with Germany, or rather with
its politics; it would have been a moral impossibility for me to write
another single word in the editorial line; so I refused the offer and
applied for sick-leave from October 1st, 1916, to the end of the war
(by telegram about the middle of August). It was granted me with
an expression of regret.

Arrived in Switzerland (February 7th, 1917), I severed all
connection with my paper by mutual consent from October 1st,
1916, onwards. After my resignation, no special editorial
representative of the Kölnische Zeitung was appointed to take my
place, as the censorship made any kind of satisfactory work
impossible.

I should like to emphasise the fact that the intrigues against me, the
crisis with Headquarters I have just mentioned, and my departure
from Constantinople did not injure me in any way either morally or
financially, and have nothing whatever to do with the present
publication. It is certainly not any petty annoyance that could bring
me to such an action, which will probably entail more than enough
unpleasant consequences for me. The reproaches levelled against
me by my pushing, jingoistic colleagues were as impotent as their
attempts to get rid of me as "dangerous to the German Cause"; I
have written proof of this from my paper in my hand, and also of

the fact that it was of my own free-will that I retired. I can therefore look forward quite calmly to all the personal invective that is sure to be showered on me for political reasons.

I had sufficient independent means not to feel the loss of my post in Constantinople too keenly; and if I still kept my post after the beginning of the crisis with Headquarters, it was simply and solely so that as a newspaper correspondent I might be in possession of fuller information, and able to follow up as long as possible the developments that were taking place on that most interesting soil of Turkey. When that was no longer possible, I refused the post offered me in Cologne—in fact twice, once by letter and once by telegram—for I could not pretend to opinions I directly opposed. I therefore remained as a free-lance in the Turkish capital. I was extremely glad that the difference of opinion ended as it did, for I had at last a free hand to say and write what I thought and felt.

My stay in Constantinople for a further three months as a silent observer naturally did not escape the notice of the German authorities, and after they had reported to the Foreign Office that a "satisfactory co-operation between me and the German representatives was not longer possible," they had of course to discover some excuse for putting an end to my prolonged stay in Turkey. They finally attempted to get rid of me by calling me up for military duty again. But this was useless in my case, for my health had been badly shaken by my spell at the Front at the beginning of the war, and besides I had the doctor's word for it that I should never be able to stand the German climate after having lived so long in the Tropics.

Whether they liked it or not, the authorities had to find some other means of getting me out of Constantinople. The Consul-General approached me, after he had discussed the matter with the Ambassador, to see if I would not like to go to Switzerland to get properly cured; otherwise he was sure I would be turned out by the Turks. They were evidently afraid, for I was getting more and more into bad odour with the German authorities for my ill-concealed opinions, that I would publish my impressions, with documentary support, as soon as ever there was a change of government in Turkey, or as soon as the German censorship was removed and anything of the kind was possible. They apparently thought that the frontier regulations would be quite sufficient to prevent my taking any documentary evidence with me to Switzerland.

As a matter of fact this was the case, and the day before my departure from Constantinople I carefully burned the whole of my many notes, which would have produced a much more effective indictment against the moral sordidness of the German-Young Turkish system than these very general sketches. But the strictest frontier regulations could not prevent me from taking with me, free of all censorship, the impressions I had received in Turkey, and the opinions I had arrived at after a painful battle for loyalty to myself as a German and to the duties I had undertaken. Even then I had considerable difficulty in getting across the frontier, and I had to wait seventeen whole days at the frontier before I was finally allowed into Switzerland. It was only owing to the fact that I sent a telegram to the Chancellor, on the authority of the Consul-General in Constantinople, begging that no difficulties of a political kind might be placed in the way of my going to Switzerland, as I had been permitted to do so by medical certificate, the passport authorities and the local command, that I finally won my point with the frontier authorities and was permitted to cross into Switzerland.

To tell the truth, I must admit that the high civil authorities, and particularly the Foreign Office, treated me throughout most kindly and courteously. For this one reason I had a hard fight with myself, right up to the very last, even after I arrived in Switzerland, before I sat down and wrote out my impressions and opinions of German-Turkish politics. And if I have now finally decided to make them public, I can only do so with an expression of the most honest regret that my private and political conscience has not allowed me to requite the kindness of the authorities by keeping silent about what I saw of the German and Turkish system.

www.ingramcontent.com/pod-product-compliance
Lightning Source LLC
Chambersburg PA
CBHW030016290326
41934CB00005B/366